D1391382
Bunty's got a brand new pic,
Now who's it going to be?
There's no room for another one.
Her walls are full, you see.

Bunty
FOR GIRLS

PRODUCED BY
The Bunty Staff

DIRECTED BY
The Ed

AND STARRING...

SUPER STORIES

Page
5 The Four Marys
13 Wendy's Winners
17 Prize Pupil
22 The Comp — a specially written story
24 Step Back In Time
29 Grappling Gertie
33 Fay's Best Friend
42 Christmas Wishes
48 Bunty — A Girl Like You
49 Marie's Magic Whistle
58 The Four Marys
65 A Family Heirloom
70 Sarah's Songbird
75 Mum For A Week
81 Luv, Lisa
90 Front Page News
96 Bunty — A Girl Like You
97 Mabel And Veronica — The Third Form Snobs
103 Holly's Holiday
109 Trick or Treat?
113 Phantom Pony
118 The Comp

FAB FEATURES

Page
40 Having A Ball!
64 Tree-Mendous!
74 Christmas Keep-Fit!
88 Stars Of St K's!
94 Lisa's Diary
108 Does Christmas Drive You Crackers?

CARTOONS

Page
21 Toots
57 Haggis
86 Bugsy and Friends

Printed and Published in Great Britain by D. C. THOMSON & CO., LTD., 185 Fleet Street, London EC4A 2HS.

ISBN 0 - 85116 - 557 - 5

The FOUR MARYS
CLOSED
MRS BURNLEY, WE NEED MORE BALLOONS URGENTLY!
AND I HAVE TO HAVE ONE OF YOUR JOKE MOUSTACHES.
WITH only a few days to go until the end of the Christmas term, the girls of St Elmo's were getting into the party spirit — especially The Four Marys.
WHY ON EARTH DO YOU WANT A FALSE MOUSTACHE?
FANCY DRESS
FOR ZE FANCY DRESS DO, MADAME. I GO AS ZE FRENCH ONION SELLER!
FALSE MOUSTACHE
I STILL DON'T KNOW WHAT TO GO AS, FIELDY.
ONE OF YOUR GIRLS LEFT THIS GLOVE HERE. THE NAME J. PHILLIPS IS INSIDE.
SANTA
THANKS. SHE'S ONE OF OUR FIRST YEARS.
IF ALL THE PROPERTY LOST BY OUR FIRST YEARS WAS GATHERED TOGETHER, IT WOULD FILL A LARGE SACK.
HEY, THANKS, SIMPY! YOU'VE JUST GIVEN ME A GREAT IDEA FOR MY FANCY DRESS. DON'T ASK WHAT — IT'S GOING TO BE A SURPRISE.

That evening —
THIS IS A BRILLIANT PARTY. I WISH COTTY WOULD HURRY UP. SHE'S MISSING ALL THE FUN.
THE SNOW MAKES YOU FEEL REALLY CHRISTMASSY.
HEY, LOOK — SANTA CLAUS HAS JUST HURRIED ACROSS FROM THE DIRECTION OF THE MAIN GATE.
I DON'T SEE ANYTHING.
But, a few minutes later —
HO! HO! HO! MERRY CHRISTMAS, EVERYONE!
I RECOGNISE THAT FACE BEHIND THE WHISKERS!
SO I DIDN'T IMAGINE THAT I SAW SANTA.
NICE COSTUME, COTTY — BUT YOU SHOULDN'T HAVE EATEN SO MUCH AT TEA. YOU'VE PUT ON AT LEAST THREE STONE.
STOP PRODDING. THOSE ARE CUSHIONS, AS WELL YOU KNOW.
THE SNOW'S FALLING QUITE HEAVILY OUTSIDE. FUNNY THAT YOUR COSTUME DIDN'T GET WET.
BUT I'VE NOT BEEN OUTSIDE. I GOT CHANGED IN THE DRAMA WARDROBE, WHERE I BORROWED THE SANTA OUTFIT FROM!
BUT I SAW YOU.
NEVER MIND THAT NOW. IS JENNY PHILLIPS HERE? AND THERE'S A PARCEL WITH PENNY DIMWORTH'S NAME ON TOO.
BRILL! SANTA'S GOT PRESSIES FOR US.

MY MISSING GLOVE!
MY HOCKEY SOCKS! I'VE NOT BEEN ABLE TO FIND THEM FOR AGES.
There were 'presents' for most of the First Years.
OUR TEDDY MASCOT. HE'S BEEN MISSING FOR OVER A MONTH.
I FOUND *HIM* STUFFED DOWN KATHY PRESTON'S LOST WELLIE BOOT, WHICH IS ALSO SOMEWHERE IN MY SACK!
NOW I SEE WHY OUR REMARK ABOUT A SACKFUL OF LOST PROPERTY GAVE YOU THIS IDEA — ER — SANTA.
SNIFF! I'VE A TICKLE IN MY NOSE. BETTER POP UP TO THE DORM FOR A TISSUE.
Upstairs —
THAT'S COTTY. WHERE'S SHE OFF TO?
HEY, YOU GOT BACK DOWNSTAIRS QUICKLY. WHAT WERE YOU DOING UP THERE? LOOKING FOR A CHIMNEY, I SUPPOSE!
I DON'T KNOW WHAT YOU'RE ON ABOUT, SIMPY. I'VE NOT LEFT THE HALL. ASK ANYONE!
POOR OLD SIMPY'S GOT SANTA ON THE BRAIN.

Much later —
THAT WAS THE BEST CHRISTMAS PARTY EVER, MISS CREEF!
I'D LIKE SOME OF YOU TO START CLEARING UP WHILE I MAKE SURE THE YOUNGER ONES GET TO BED. FIELD — YOU CAN HELP ME.
MISS CREEF, WE'VE JUST SEEN SANTA CLAUS — THE *REAL* ONE.
WE CAME ROUND THE CORNER AND THERE HE WAS. WHEN HE SAW US, HE CLIMBED OUT OF THE WINDOW.
DON'T BE RIDICULOUS. GO TO BED AT ONCE. FIELD — CLOSE THAT WINDOW.
THE SNOW ON THE ROOF HAS BEEN DISTURBED, AS IF SOMEONE REALLY HAS BEEN OUT ON THE ROOF. I HOPE IT WASN'T ONE OF THE FIRST YEARS FOOLING AROUND.
A little later —
THE FIRST YEARS THOUGHT THEY SAW SANTA CLAUS. NOW MAYBE YOU'LL BELIEVE THAT *I* WASN'T IMAGINING THINGS.
GOOD GRACIOUS — WHAT A VERY FINE OIL PAINTING, MISS CREEF. WHERE DID IT COME FROM?
IT'S — IT'S CALLED 'THE REARING HORSE' BY JOSEPH PALLINI, MISS MITCHELL. IT WAS BEQUEATHED TO THE SCHOOL BY A FORMER GOVERNOR.

WHY HAVE I NEVER SEEN IT BEFORE?
IT ALWAYS USED TO HANG IN THIS VERY SPOT, HEADMISTRESS — BUT IT WAS STOLEN IN A BURGLARY JUST BEFORE YOU CAME HERE.
MISS WESTON — YOU LOOK LIKE YOU'VE SEEN A GHOST.
I'VE CERTAINLY JUST SEEN SOMETHING WHICH I THOUGHT HAD GONE FOREVER — THE DELIMEAD CUP, WHICH WAS STOLEN FROM THE TROPHY CUPBOARD.
LOOK — THERE IT IS.
IT WAS STOLEN AT THE SAME TIME AS THE PALLINI PAINTING!
I REMEMBER THE BURGLARY, ALTHOUGH WE WERE ONLY FIRST YEARS AT THE TIME. DIDN'T A RATHER SPECIAL BOOK GO MISSING FROM THE LIBRARY TOO?
INDEED, RADLEIGH! IT WAS A FIRST EDITION.
LET'S SEE IF IT HAS RE-APPEARED TOO.
I DO HOPE SO.
THERE'S NO SIGN OF IT. IT WAS TOO MUCH TO HOPE FOR.
IT STILL DOESN'T EXPLAIN HOW AND WHY THE OTHER STOLEN ITEMS HAVE BEEN RETURNED.
OH WELL, LET'S ALL GET TO BED AND WORRY ABOUT IT IN THE MORNING.

BATHROOM
WHAT'S WRONG, SIMPY?
LOOK AT THESE FOOTPRINTS. THERE'S EVEN SOME FRESH SNOW HERE.

COME ON, LET'S FOLLOW THE TRAIL.

LOOK!
FIELDY — RUN AND FETCH HELP. WE'LL WAIT OUTSIDE THE DOOR AND MAKE SURE HE DOESN'T GIVE US THE SLIP AGAIN.

SSSH! HE'S STILL IN YOUR STUDY, MISS MITCHELL.
OH, DEAR! HE'S PROBABLY BREAKING INTO MY SAFE.

STRESS
CHARGE!

GOOD GRACIOUS — A GIRL!

THE FIRST EDITION!
I WAS PUTTING IT BACK, ONLY I WASN'T SURE WHERE IT HAD BEEN STOLEN FROM. I THOUGHT I'D TRY AND PUT IT IN THE SAFE.

DID YOU REPLACE THE OTHER STOLEN ITEMS, MY DEAR? DON'T BE FRIGHTENED. JUST TELL US.
YOU CERTAINLY OWE US AN EXPLANATION. FOR A START, WHO ARE YOU?

I'M CHRISSIE LONG. MY GRANDFATHER FELL SERIOUSLY ILL SOME MONTHS AGO AND I WENT TO NURSE HIM. HE CONFESSED TO ME THAT WHEN HIS BUSINESS WAS IN TROUBLE, HE WAS DOING SOME BUILDING WORK IN THIS SCHOOL. ON IMPULSE, HE STOLE THE PAINTING, THE BOOK AND THE CUP TO SELL!

THEN, HE REALISED JUST HOW WRONG IT WAS, AND KEPT THE THINGS HIDDEN, TRYING TO THINK OF A WAY OF RETURNING THEM. WITH JUST A FEW DAYS TO LIVE, HE ASKED ME TO DO IT FOR HIM. I PROMISED, AND HE DIED WITH AN EASIER CONSCIENCE.

FOR MONTHS, I WONDERED HOW TO RETURN THOSE THINGS WITHOUT INCRIMINATING MYSELF OR GRANDFATHER. THEN WHEN I HEARD ABOUT YOUR FANCY DRESS PARTY, I SAW IT AS A WAY OF GETTING INTO THE SCHOOL.

WILL YOU CALL THE POLICE NOW?
THAT IS UP TO THE HEADMISTRESS — BUT I DON'T QUITE SEE WHAT YOU COULD BE CHARGED WITH. YOU WERE RETURNING PROPERTY — NOT TAKING IT AWAY.

MISS CREEF IS GOING TO DRIVE CHRISSIE HOME. POOR CHILD — WHAT SHE DID WAS WRONG, BUT SHE SHOWED WONDERFUL LOYALTY TO HER GRANDFATHER.
OH DEAR, WHAT A PITY! I WAS ACTUALLY BEGINNING TO BELIEVE THAT IT REALLY WAS SANTA CLAUS.
PERHAPS A NICE CUP OF HOT CHOCOLATE WOULD MAKE UP FOR IT, BEFORE YOU GO TO BED.
When the Marys finally got to their dormitory —
SOME IDIOT'S LEFT THE WINDOW WIDE OPEN. IT'S FREEZING IN HERE.
SSSH! EVERYONE ELSE IS FAST ASLEEP.
SOMEONE'S PUT A PARCEL ON MY BED.
WE'VE *ALL* GOT ONE.
OUR FAVOURITE CHOCS!
WHO ARE THEY FROM? WE'VE BEEN WITH MADDY MITCHELL, SO IT COULDN'T HAVE BEEN HER.
PERHAPS IT'S A THANK YOU FROM CHRISSIE?
BUT CREEFY'S TAKING CHRISSIE HOME. IT COULDN'T HAVE BEEN HER.
ER . . . GIRLS . . . DON'T LAUGH, BUT YOU DON'T THINK IT MIGHT HAVE BEEN . . . DO YOU . . . ?
THE END

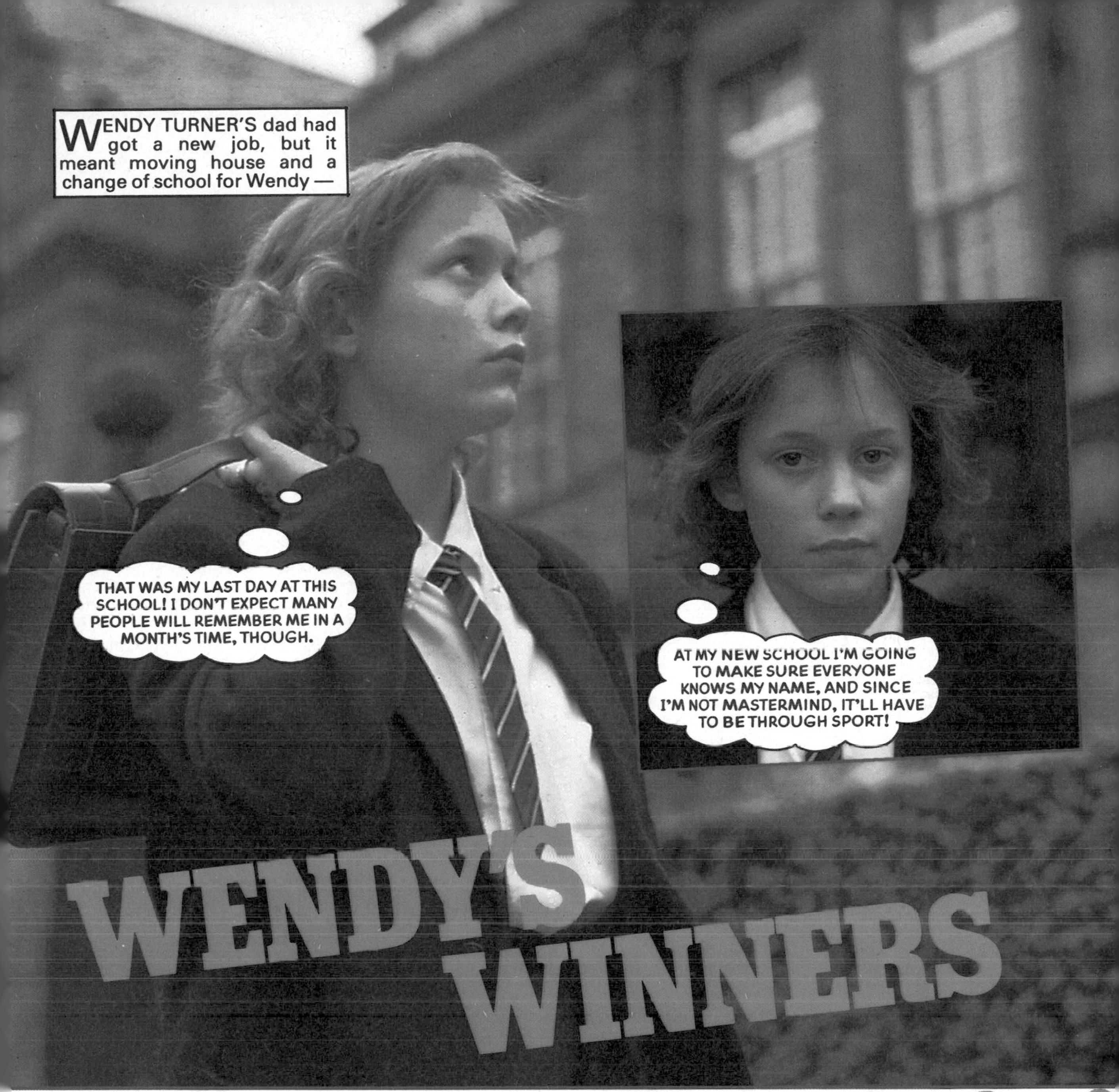

WENDY TURNER'S dad had got a new job, but it meant moving house and a change of school for Wendy —

THAT WAS MY LAST DAY AT THIS SCHOOL! I DON'T EXPECT MANY PEOPLE WILL REMEMBER ME IN A MONTH'S TIME, THOUGH.

AT MY NEW SCHOOL I'M GOING TO MAKE SURE EVERYONE KNOWS MY NAME, AND SINCE I'M NOT MASTERMIND, IT'LL HAVE TO BE THROUGH SPORT!

WENDY'S WINNERS

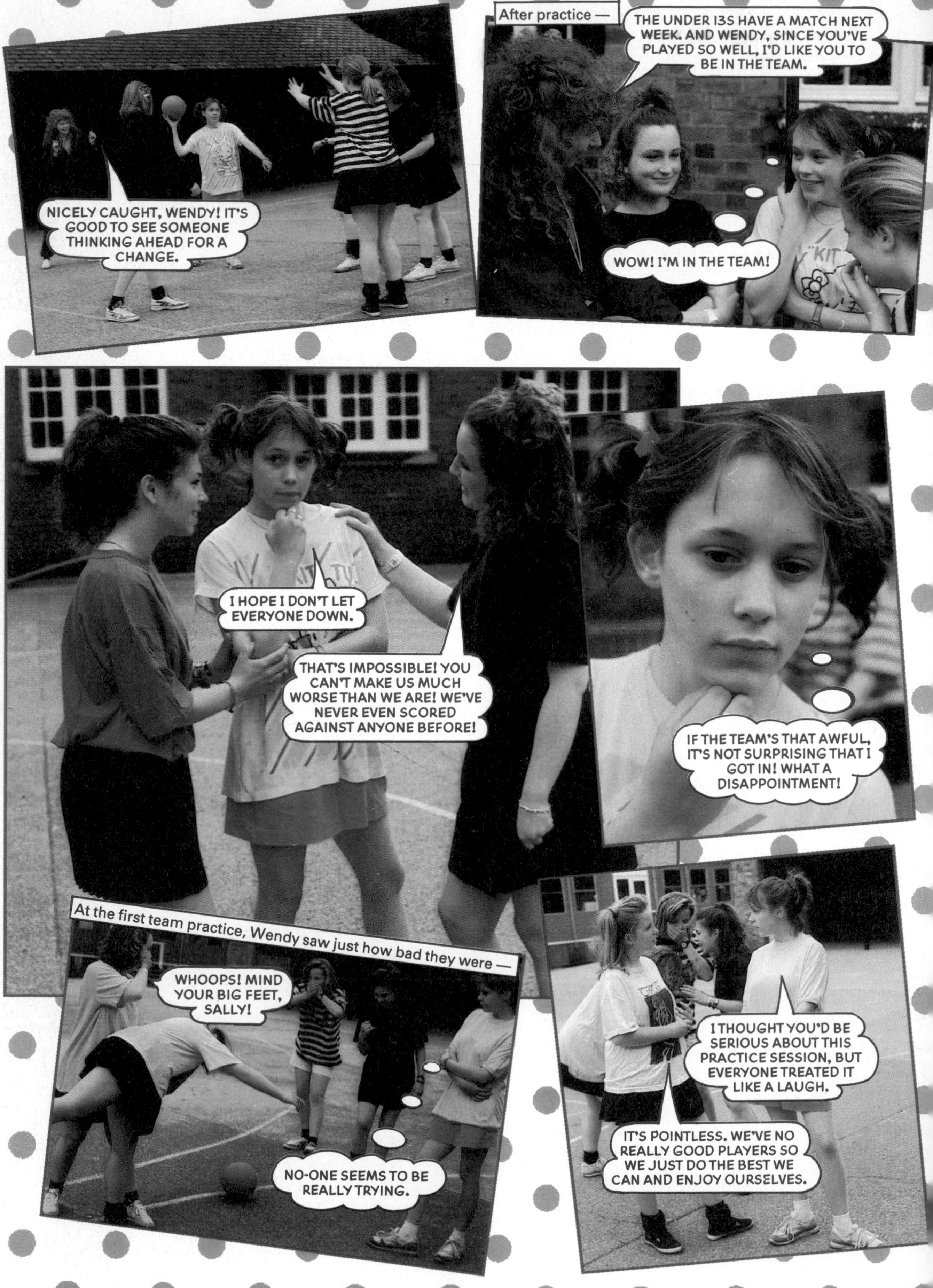

I HOPE I DON'T LET EVERYONE DOWN.

THAT'S IMPOSSIBLE! YOU CAN'T MAKE US MUCH WORSE THAN WE ARE! WE'VE NEVER EVEN SCORED AGAINST ANYONE BEFORE!

IF THE TEAM'S THAT AWFUL, IT'S NOT SURPRISING THAT I GOT IN! WHAT A DISAPPOINTMENT!

At the first team practice, Wendy saw just how bad they were —

WHOOPS! MIND YOUR BIG FEET, SALLY!

NO-ONE SEEMS TO BE REALLY TRYING.

I THOUGHT YOU'D BE SERIOUS ABOUT THIS PRACTICE SESSION, BUT EVERYONE TREATED IT LIKE A LAUGH.

IT'S POINTLESS. WE'VE NO REALLY GOOD PLAYERS SO WE JUST DO THE BEST WE CAN AND ENJOY OURSELVES.

JUST ONCE, WOULDN'T YOU LIKE TO KNOW WHAT IT FEELS LIKE, TO COME OUT ON TOP?
IT WOULD MAKE A CHANGE — ESPECIALLY PLAYING THAT BIG-HEADED HIGHCLIFF CROWD.
THEN WHY NOT DO SOMETHING ABOUT IT? LET'S PRACTISE HARD AND SEE IF IT HELPS. I DON'T KNOW ABOUT YOU, BUT I WANT TO WIN!
IF IT MEANS THAT MUCH TO YOU, I DON'T MIND GIVING IT A GO.
So —
WHAT? YOU WANT US TO JOG ROUND THE PARK EVERY NIGHT? YOU'RE NOT SERIOUS.
OH YES, I AM. AND AFTER THIS WE'LL DO SOME SHOOTING PRACTICE.
GO FOR IT, SANDY! SEE IF YOU CAN GET TEN OUT OF TEN!
EVERYONE'S DOING WELL AND TRYING HARD. MAYBE WE *CAN* WIN!
And by their next team practice —
I CAN'T BELIEVE THIS! YOU'RE IMPROVING, GIRLS.
IF MISS TRENCHER'S NOTICED THE DIFFERENCE, THEN WE MUST BE GETTING BETTER.
On the day of the game against Highcliff —
COME ON, GIRLS, WE'RE GOING TO GIVE THE OPPOSITION A TOUGH TIME.
HERE ARE THE ALL-TIME LOSERS! WAS IT 16-0 WE BEAT THEM LAST TIME?
IGNORE THEM. WE'VE BEEN TRAINING HARD. THIS TIME IT'LL BE DIFFERENT!

But —
THEY'RE RUNNING RINGS ROUND US — WE'VE ONLY SCORED TWO GOALS. SO MUCH FOR MY DREAMS OF BEING ON A WINNING TEAM!
And, finally —
YES! HIGHCLIFF WINS 15-2!
SORRY, WENDY, BUT I WARNED YOU THAT HIGHCLIFF WOULD TRAMPLE US INTO THE GROUND!
YOU PLAYED WELL, SANDY! IT WASN'T YOUR FAULT THAT YOUR OPPONENT WAS SO QUICK. ONCE WENDY'S GOT US ALL FIT YOU'LL DO EVEN BETTER.
SHAME WE LOST, BUT IT WAS GOOD FUN.
YEAH, I REALLY ENJOYED MYSELF. THANKS TO GOOD OLD WENDY'S TRAINING, AT LEAST WE DID SCORE TWO!
TELL YOU WHAT, LET'S HAVE A LOSERS' PARTY AT MY PLACE.
THAT'S THE BEST IDEA YET.
Later —
OH, WELL. AT LEAST I'LL BE REMEMBERED AS A MEMBER OF THE FIRST DEEPDALE NETBALL TEAM TO SCORE IN A MATCH!
HERE'S TO WENDY!
JUST WAIT TILL OUR NEXT MATCH. THAT WILL BE EVEN MORE FUN 'COS WE'LL BE *WINNERS*!!
THE END

PRIZE PUPIL

NEW girl, Marie Brown, joined Chepley School at the beginning of the summer term —
THIS IS MARIE BROWN, CLASS. YOU'RE JUST IN TIME FOR OUR SCHOOL'S ANNUAL OPEN DAY, MARIE. WE HAVE A TRADITION AT CHEPLEY THAT THE PUPIL WHO ENCOURAGES THE MOST PEOPLE TO COME WINS A PRIZE!
SUE AND KATE, FOR EXAMPLE, ARE DOING A SPONSORED POT-IN. THEY'RE GOING TO MAKE AS MANY THINGS AS THEY CAN IN AN HOUR ON THE SCHOOL'S POTTERY WHEEL. ALL THEIR FRIENDS AND RELATIONS ARE COMING TO WATCH THEM.
WHY DON'T YOU JOIN THEM, MARIE? YOU SHOULD BE INVOLVED WITH SOMETHING, AND IT'S A BIT LATE TO THINK OF A PLAN OF YOUR OWN.
WELL, I'LL TRY, MISS CARTER.
So, later—
EM . . . I'VE NEVER ACTUALLY DONE POTTERY BEFORE.
IT'S QUITE EASY, MARIE. FIRST YOU HAVE TO CENTRE YOUR CLAY.

But—
KEEP THE WHEEL GOING!
OH, DEAR — WHAT A MESS!
EM . . . I DON'T THINK I'M QUITE CUT OUT FOR POTTERY. I THINK I'D BETTER TRY SOMETHING ELSE.
So—
HOW ABOUT JOINING THE GYM SQUAD? WE'RE PUTTING ON A DISPLAY IN THE HALL ON OPEN DAY. LOTS OF OUR FRIENDS WANT TO COME AND WATCH.
OKAY! THANKS, JILL!
Marie went along—
YOUR TURN, MARIE.
AAAH!
CRUMBS — SHE'S KNOCKED EVERYONE OVER!
Later, in the English class—
PERHAPS YOU WOULD LIKE TO JOIN THE DRAMA GROUP, MARIE? WE'RE PERFORMING PIECES FROM SHAKESPEARE ON OPEN DAY.
I'LL GIVE IT A GO, MISS EVANS.
But at the rehearsal—
WHEREFORE ART THOU . . . ERM . . . OH, DEAR, I'VE FORGOTTEN YOUR NAME!
IT'S ROMEO! YOU'RE JULIET AND I'M ROMEO. HOW CAN YOU FORGET THAT?

WHOOPS! I DON'T THINK MARIE'S GOING TO LAST LONG IN THE DRAMA GROUP.
TOO RIGHT, EMMA. SHE'LL SCARE PEOPLE AWAY FROM THE OPEN DAY — INSTEAD OF ENCOURAGING THEM TO COME! SHE'LL HAVE TO DO SOMETHING ELSE.
Marie joined the cookery demonstration team. But—
OH, NO — WHERE DID I GO WRONG? MY SPONGE IS AS FLAT AS A PANCAKE!
I THINK BAKED BEANS ON TOAST IS MORE YOUR LINE, MARIE.
And later—
SHE CAN'T RUN FAST EITHER. THE RELAY SQUAD WILL RECORD THEIR SLOWEST EVER TIME IF *SHE* TAKES PART! *THAT* ISN'T GOING TO ENCOURAGE PEOPLE TO COME AND WATCH.
So, in registration class—
I'M SORRY, MARIE. I FEEL IT MIGHT BE BETTER IF YOU FORGOT ABOUT DOING ANYTHING TO ENCOURAGE VISITORS TO OUR OPEN DAY.
JUST AS WELL. SHE'S HOPELESS.
THAT'S A PITY. I WANTED TO HELP MY NEW SCHOOL. I'LL INVITE MUM AND DAD ALONG, OF COURSE, BUT I WANTED TO ENCOURAGE SOME OTHERS. OH! I KNOW!
On Open Day—
OPEN DAY
I'VE BROUGHT TWENTY PEOPLE ALONG TO WATCH ME MAKE POTS!
KAREN WALSH HAS BROUGHT THIRTY-THREE TO SEE HER IN THE GYMNASTIC DISPLAY. I THINK THAT PUTS HER IN THE LEAD.

But then—
DAY
NOT ANY MORE! LOOK OVER THERE! THERE ARE *HUNDREDS* COMING IN!
WHO'S BROUGHT THEM?

OH! IT'S MARIE BROWN! HOW ON EARTH DID SHE DO IT?

TELL US, MARIE. WHAT DID YOU DO TO PERSUADE ALL THOSE PEOPLE TO COME TO OUR SCHOOL'S OPEN DAY?
WELL, IT WAS EASY! DAD AND I JUST WALKED ROUND TOWN TOGETHER SAYING IN LOUD VOICES THAT WE WERE COMING TO THE CHEPLEY OPEN DAY, AND A HUGE CROWD FOLLOWED US!

BUT I DON'T UNDERSTAND! WHY SHOULD ANYONE FOLLOW *YOU?*
WELL, MAYBE IT'S BECAUSE OF MY DAD . . .

DID I FORGET TO MENTION IT? HE'S STEVE SPARKLE, THE POP STAR! EVERYBODY'S HOPING FOR HIS AUTOGRAPH OR THE CHANCE TO SPEAK TO HIM!
WOW! STEVE SPARKLE'S MARIE'S DAD! I DON'T BELIEVE IT!

AT THE LAST COUNT, THERE WERE ONE HUNDRED AND TWENTY OF THEM. LOOKS LIKE I'LL WIN THE PRIZE FOR ENCOURAGING THE MOST PEOPLE TO THE FETE AFTER ALL!
THE END

TOOTS
OH, THAT DOG'S RUNNING AWAY!
HEY — COME BACK!
NOW HE'S JUMPED THE FENCE!
YUGH — IT'S ALL MUDDY!
HE'S JUMPED RIGHT OVER THAT STREAM!
HA! HA! YOU ALMOST MADE IT, TOOTS!
I'M NOT GIVING UP. COME BACK HERE!
WHERE'S HE OFF TO NOW? WE'RE IN THE WOODS!
?
GOTCHA!
MAYBE I'LL GET A REWARD FOR ALL MY TROUBLE . . .
YES?
I'VE BROUGHT YOUR DOG BACK!
HE'S NOT MY DOG. I CHASED HIM OFF THIS MORNING. HE KEEPS COMING INTO MY GARDEN!
HUH! SOME REWARD!
SILLY TOOTS!

The COMP

A SPECIALLY WRITTEN STORY

HI, girls! Laura here — Laura Brady. Our school's about to break up for the Christmas hols — that's Redvale Comprehensive, by the way, known as The Comp — or, if you look at some of the pupils — namely, Hodge and Freddy — the Chamber of Horrors!

Well, anyway, I'm writing this to tell you about our Lower School Christmas Concert. Yeah, I know, yawn, yawn! That's what we thought, too, when we started rehearsing for it. Actually, it didn't turn out to be too bad — at least, once Miss Walton took over.

I'll explain. She replaced our old Music teacher, "Groaner" Jackson, at half term, when Groaner left to have a nervous breakdown caused by our lovely singing. Only kidding — actually she moved to another job. At first, we didn't think much of Miss Walton. Rather a lot of fuzzy hair, specs, a bit on the skinny side, you know? Becky (that's my best friend) said she was sure she'd seen her somewhere before, but the rest of us didn't think so. She was just one of those real ordinary people, you know? Just another teacher. *DOUBLE* yawn.

Groaner had arranged the concert — the first year recorder group (painful!), a few kids doing piano solos or what-have-you, and then us, the third years, giving an utterly brilliant rendition of some olde-worlde folksongs. Exciting stuff, eh?

Hayley — that's Becky's twin — said once Miss Walton took over, things might get better. But we didn't see how. All music teachers absolutely love boring old folksongs, don't they? So we weren't hoping for too much improvement.

The first rehearsal with Miss Walton started off as usual. We laboured our way through a couple of sea shanties, and wailed "D'Ye Ken John Peel". Then, when I glanced over at her, I noticed Miss Walton looking as bored as we were.

Halfway through "Molly Malone", she stopped us by rapping on the top of the piano.

"Oh, dear," she sighed. "Can't you put a bit more life into it than that?"

Hodge snorted and muttered that you couldn't put life into a song that'd been dead for hundreds of years. Miss Walton must have heard him.

"I'll show you," she said.

And she really did, too! Talk about letting your hair down! She stood up at the piano like a proper keyboard player, whipped her specs off, and ripped out a jazzed up version that got us really grooving.

"See?" she smiled at the end of it.

"Radical," I said. "Like a real singer!"

Suddenly Becky gasped.

"That's it, Laura. She *IS* a real singer. She used to be with that band, Total Sounds! You did, didn't you, miss?"

Miss Walton laughed and admitted it.

We were amazed! A real pop singer, teaching us! If she was a pop star, why on earth give it up to teach at the boring, old Comp? I wouldn't have! But according to her, it was for the job security. And anyway, Total Sounds had disbanded a while ago, and she needed work.

Well, we'd lost all interest in folksongs, even jazzed-up ones! We pleaded with her to sing, "Ready For Your Love", Total Sounds' last hit. And she did. Better than that, she enjoyed it so much she agreed to teach us the song for our concert — and other Total Sounds' songs, too!

Then Hodge thought of

something.

"Bet she's got contacts in the records biz," he said, as we filed out of the hall after rehearsal.

"So?" we wanted to know.

He hung back to wait for Miss Walton. We waited, too.

"Miss — any chance you could get us a recording session?"

Miss Walton laughed.

"From what I heard back there, you'd need to improve rather a lot, David! But . . . I don't know. If you work really hard on the concert, I'll have a word at the studios where we used to record, and . . ."

We didn't hear the rest 'cos of our shouts and whooping!

Well, for the next few weeks, did we ever work hard! Miss Walton taught us a couple of songs she'd just written, which had never been performed before — they were crucial! She let Hodge and Freddy play guitar and drums. Once she'd licked them into shape, it didn't sound too bad!

Only one problem. Her Grimness. Our high and mighty Head, Grim Gertie Grimstyle. We all knew Gertie's opinion on what she called *"MODERN* music". So, one lunch hour when she popped into the hall to hear us halfway through "Ready For Your Love", her face would've stopped every clock in the school.

"Miss Walton, a word with you, please!" she snapped. "I was under the impression that this was a rehearsal for the lower school concert!"

Miss Walton said that it was. Gertie's voice grew icier.

"I understood that the third form choir was to be performing folksongs. Kindly see to it that they do!"

There was a dead hush when she swept off.

"We're not going to, are we, miss?" Freddy asked. "After all our rehearsing?"

"Of course we are," said Miss Walton. "Miss Grimstyle wants it, and she's the Head."

A chorus of groans went up. Miss Walton held up a hand.

"We shall sing a couple of folksongs — just to keep Miss Grimstyle happy. But we didn't promise we wouldn't sing our songs too, did we?"

Loud cheers! She was definitely all right, was Miss Walton!

We practised dead hard and gave it everything, after that. And the week before the concert, Miss Walton gave us some knockout news.

She'd only gone and booked a recording studio for the next Saturday!

"Wow! Us, recording stars! We're gonna be famous!" whooped Roz.

Hodge and Freddy, as backing musicians, thought it was all due to their talent. They offered to sell us their autographs for fifty pence apiece. Needless to say, we didn't take them up on it.

So we all trouped into the studio. It was amazing! We were shown around the studio, and then we had to sing in the soundproof booth. We went through the song about four times before the engineer got the sound he wanted. Then he played it back to us. It sounded wicked!

We sang another song, one of Miss Walton's own, for the other side of the tape, and when we left the studios we really felt like big time singing stars! Hodge and Freddy had upped the asking price for their autographs to a pound, but Hodge said he wasn't going to let fame change him. I said no, he'd still be a berk, and then I had to run for it!

Well, the day of the concert dawned. I have to say, I was a teensy bit worried and so were the twins and Roz. I mean — there was still the Gertie problem. Her Grimness was about to find out that we'd altered the programme! What if she stopped us?

The younger kids went on first, and did their stuff — and then it was our turn.

Gertie frowned a bit when we did our jazzed-up version of "Molly Malone". But when we launched into "Ready For Your Love", wow, her *FACE!* It turned to *STONE!*

But the audience loved us! They roared and stamped their approval, and Gertie had to let us continue. By our third song, we had them clapping along. We had to do two encores and three curtain calls! And we made sure Miss Walton took a special bow, as the writer of most of our songs. The audience almost clapped their hands off!

But Gertie still looked furious. And first thing next day she summoned Miss Walton to her office.

We waited outside, anxiously, but Miss Walton came out smiling.

"Did she eat you alive, miss?" Becky asked.

"At first," said Miss Walton.

"But when I showed her this —" she produced a cassette tape of our recording "— and told her there are five hundred copies which can go on sale at, say, two pounds each for the School Funds . . . well, she melted quite quickly. She's delighted with the whole idea!"

"Does that mean we can do *more* modern music?" asked Hodge.

But Miss Walton shook her head.

"Not with me, I'm afraid. You see — I'm leaving the Comp."

We all cried out in protest. We thought it was something Grim Gertie had said to her. But no, performing in public and hearing the applause had made Miss Walton realise that she really missed the music business — and so she's going back into it after Christmas, as a solo artist.

You can bet we'll be watching out for her!

So we've lost the best music teacher we've ever had. But I can't say I blame her. If you offered me the choice between teaching and being a pop star, I know which I'd choose!

By the way. Anyone want to buy a tape of some really cool sounds? Only two quid — a real bargain. And I promise I won't let Hodge autograph it. Deal?

Uh-oh — he's sneaked up on me and he's been reading over my shoulder! Er — me, call you a berk, Hodge? Now, would I?

See you, girls! Time I wasn't here!

THE END

Step Back In Time

LUCY WILKS and her parents were looking round Hardfast Mills, a working museum.

WHEN YOU SAID WE'D VISIT A MUSEUM FOR A DAY, I THOUGHT IT'D BE DULL, BUT THIS IS TERRIFIC. IT'S LIKE STEPPING BACK IN TIME.

IT'S FAR MORE INTERESTING SEEING PEOPLE ACTING THE PARTS OF THE WORKERS WHO USED TO BE HERE.

THIS IS BORING! MUM AND DAD HAVE DOZED OFF. I THINK I'LL TAKE A CLOSER LOOK AT THE APPRENTICES' HOUSE.

A few minutes later —
WHAT'S THIS? A SCHOOL OUTING?

BEEN A GOOD DAY, AIN'T IT, SAMMY?
LIKE HEAVEN! I WENT DOWN BY THE RIVER AND JUST SLEPT.

ANOTHER YEAR UNTIL OUR NEXT DAY OUT. SEEMS LIKE A LIFETIME.
SOME OF US MIGHT NOT MAKE IT THAT FAR. WILL'S BEEN COUGHING REAL BAD LATELY.
I GET IT! THEY'RE MORE ACTORS, PLAYING JOSIAH HARDFAST'S APPRENTICES.

HEY! MIND WHO YOU'RE SHOVING!
WE GOT TO GET BACK. MRS THRING WILL BE WAITING FOR US!

GET INSIDE, YOU IDLE BRATS!
I'M BEING SWEPT ALONG WITH THE ACTORS! I CAN'T GET OUT!

WILKS, YOU WERE TOLD TO SCRUB THE KITCHEN FLOOR THIS MORNING, BUT IT WEREN'T DONE PROPER, YOU USELESS NO-GOOD BOY!
I'M NOT A BOY!
HOW DID SHE KNOW MY NAME?

TAKE THAT SMILE OFF YOUR FACE, BOY, OR I'LL DO IT FOR YOU!
WOW! THIS ACTRESS IS REALLY SCARING ME! I THINK I'LL GO BACK OUTSIDE AND WAIT FOR MUM AND DAD.

But —
THERE'S NO HANDLE ON THE INSIDE OF THIS DOOR. CAN ONE OF YOU LET ME OUT, PLEASE?
DON'T ANNOY MRS THRING, OR SHE'LL TAKE IT OUT ON THE REST OF US.
BEST SCRUB THAT FLOOR LIKE SHE TOLD YOU, WILKS.

So —
THIS MUST ALL BE PART OF THE LIVING MUSEUM — GETTING VISITORS TO TAKE PART IN THE EXHIBITS — BUT I DON'T THINK MUCH OF IT!

Then —
WILKS, YOU IDLE CREATURE! TAKE THE GRUEL TO THE TABLE.
I'D BETTER DO AS SHE SAYS OR I'LL LOOK A REAL SPOILSPORT. I DON'T SUPPOSE IT'S A REAL CAULDRON ANYHOW.

OUCH! IT'S REAL ENOUGH! IT'S TOO HEAVY FOR ME, AND THE HANDLE'S RED HOT!
CLUMSY BRAT!

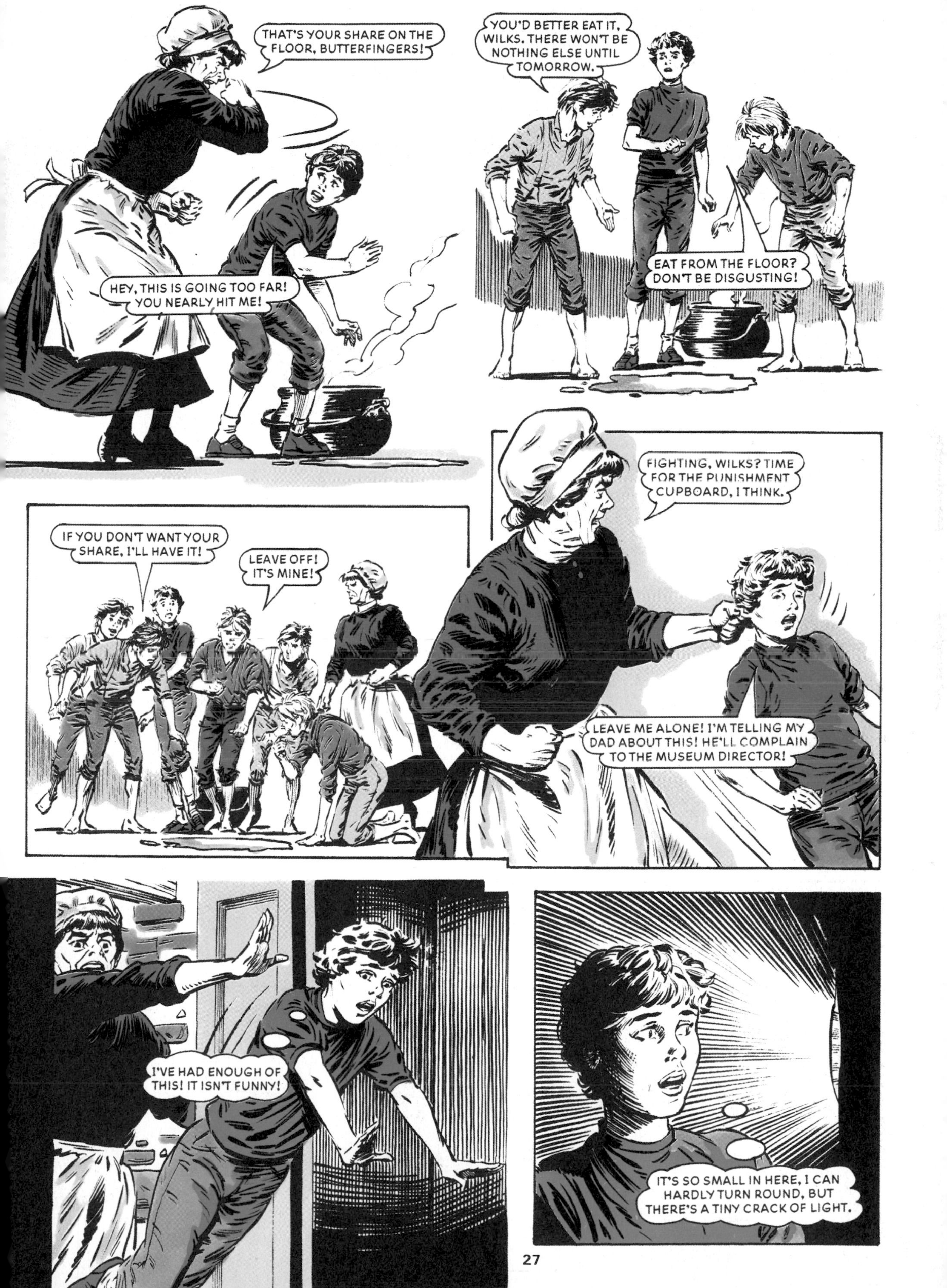

THAT'S YOUR SHARE ON THE FLOOR, BUTTERFINGERS!

HEY, THIS IS GOING TOO FAR! YOU NEARLY HIT ME!

YOU'D BETTER EAT IT, WILKS. THERE WON'T BE NOTHING ELSE UNTIL TOMORROW.

EAT FROM THE FLOOR? DON'T BE DISGUSTING!

IF YOU DON'T WANT YOUR SHARE, I'LL HAVE IT!

LEAVE OFF! IT'S MINE!

FIGHTING, WILKS? TIME FOR THE PUNISHMENT CUPBOARD, I THINK.

LEAVE ME ALONE! I'M TELLING MY DAD ABOUT THIS! HE'LL COMPLAIN TO THE MUSEUM DIRECTOR!

THERE'S MUM AND DAD LOOKING FOR ME! I'LL SHOUT AT THEM, AND THEY CAN COME AND GET ME OUT.

MUM! DAD! GET ME OUT OF HERE!
WHY CAN'T THEY HEAR ME?

Then —
WAKE UP, LOVE — IF WE'RE GOING TO LOOK AROUND THE APPRENTICES' HOUSE, WE'LL HAVE TO HURRY. THE MUSEUM CLOSES IN JUST OVER AN HOUR.
WH . . . WHAT?
IT WAS ALL A BAD DREAM! THANK GOODNESS!

SOMEONE WILL BE PLAYING THE PART OF THE APPRENTICES' HOUSE SUPERVISOR. SHE'S GOING TO SHOW US AROUND.

Inside —
I CAN'T WAIT TO SEE EVERYTHING.
IT'S MRS THRING! WHAT'S BEEN GOING ON? IT WAS JUST A DREAM — *WASN'T* IT?
THE END

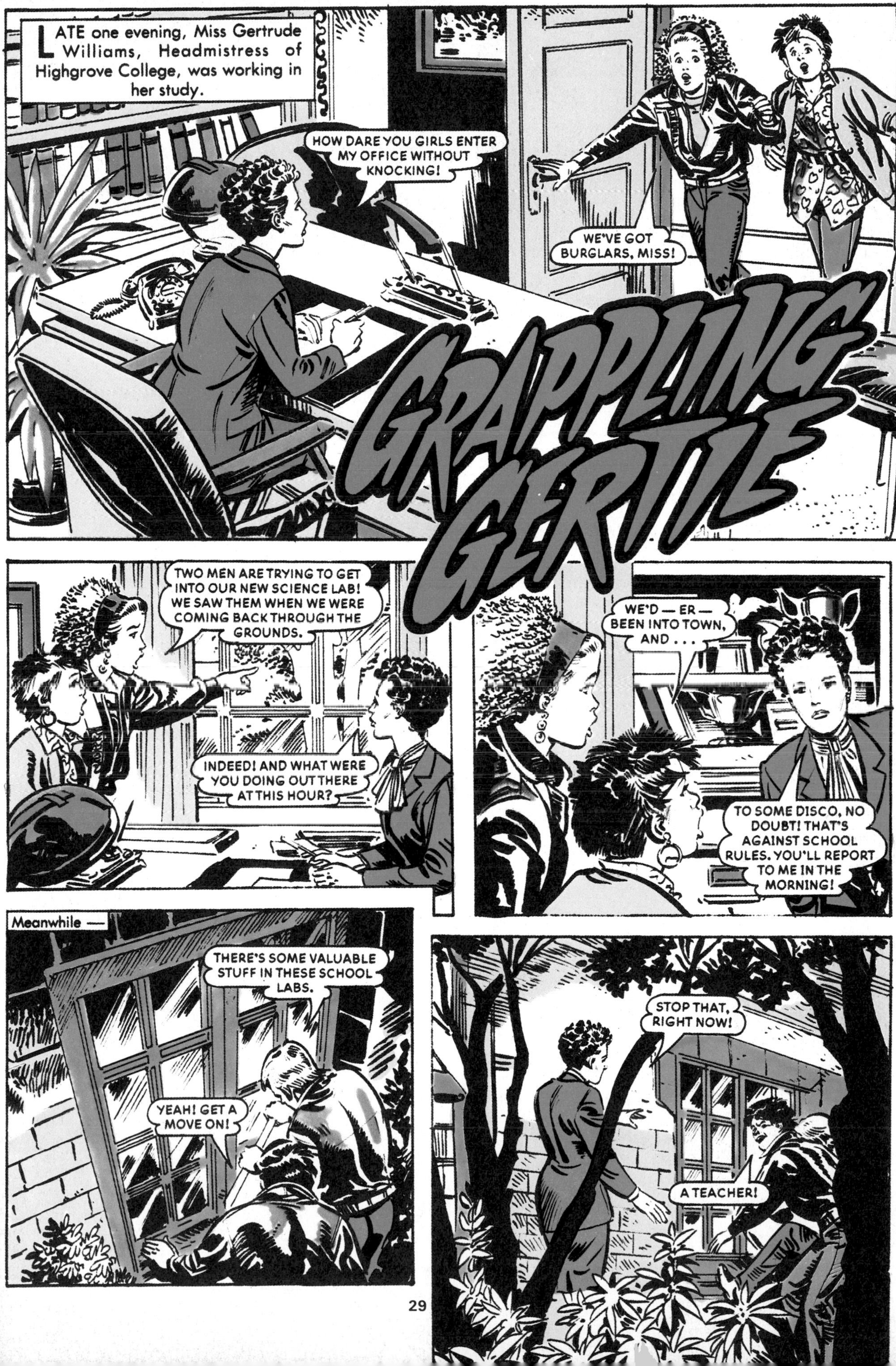

GRAPPLING GERTIE

LATE one evening, Miss Gertrude Williams, Headmistress of Highgrove College, was working in her study.

HOW DARE YOU GIRLS ENTER MY OFFICE WITHOUT KNOCKING!

WE'VE GOT BURGLARS, MISS!

TWO MEN ARE TRYING TO GET INTO OUR NEW SCIENCE LAB! WE SAW THEM WHEN WE WERE COMING BACK THROUGH THE GROUNDS.

INDEED! AND WHAT WERE YOU DOING OUT THERE AT THIS HOUR?

WE'D — ER — BEEN INTO TOWN, AND . . .

TO SOME DISCO, NO DOUBT! THAT'S AGAINST SCHOOL RULES. YOU'LL REPORT TO ME IN THE MORNING!

BACK OFF, LADY, OR YOU MIGHT GET HURT!
SOMEHOW I DON'T THINK SO, BOYS.
TAKE THAT!
OOF!
AND THAT!
AAGH!
THEY MUST TEACH WRESTLING AT THIS SCHOOL!
AND DON'T COME BACK!
I SHOULD HAVE KEPT THEM AND CALLED THE POLICE.
BUT THAT MIGHT HAVE UPSET MY PLANS FOR TONIGHT!
LEOPARD LILY RETURNS!
BUT WHO IS HER OPPONENT, I WONDER?

KRAZY KAT CLUB
Later, outside a club hall —
AH, BEAR-HUG BELINDA! A REAL RIB-CRUSHER!

In the dressing room —
YOU MIGHT HAVE CHOSEN AN EASIER OPPONENT FOR MY RETURN TO THE WRESTLING SCENE, MAX!
AS YOUR MANAGER, I HAD TO FIX A MATCH THAT WOULD PULL THE CROWDS, GERTIE.

MY APPOINTMENT AS HEADMISTRESS AT HIGHGROVE HAS KEPT ME OUT OF THE RING FOR SOME TIME, MAX. I AM ONLY RETURNING TO IT IN ORDER TO GAIN MONEY FOR SCHOOL FUNDS.

So, soon —
TEAR HER TO BITS, LIL!
THIS IS GOING TO BE TOUGH! IT'S JUST AS WELL I HAD THAT PRACTICE WITH THOSE BURGLARS!
FLATTEN HER, BELINDA!

AAAGH! GO EASY, BELINDA!
THAT'S JUST A NICE HUG TO GREET YOU BACK!

OW! MY LEGS! I THOUGHT THINGS HAD BEEN FIXED FOR ME TO WIN THIS FIGHT, BELINDA?
THAT'S TRUE, BUT WE'VE GOT TO GIVE VALUE FOR MONEY!

GOT TO PUT ON A GOOD SHOW, BELINDA!
OOF! LAY OFF THOSE SMASHES, GERTIE!
BASH HER, LIL!
LEMME GO! I GIVE IN!
A LEG-SCISSORS HOLD TOO MUCH FOR YOU, IS IT?
AND THE WINNER BY A SUBMISSION IS LEOPARD LILY!
GREAT FIGHT, BUT YOU CUT IT A BIT SHORT, DIDN'T YOU?
I HAD TO, MAX. I'M STILL RATHER OUT OF PRACTICE — AND I HAVE TO GET BACK TO SCHOOL BEFORE I'M MISSED!
At school, next morning —
LOUISE PARSONS AND SARAH JONES. FOR YOUR DISGRACEFUL BEHAVIOUR YOU ARE BOTH CONFINED TO SCHOOL QUARTERS FOR A WEEK. I WILL NOT HAVE GIRLS FROM THIS COLLEGE FREQUENTING DISCOS — YOU UNDERSTAND?
YES, MISS. SORRY, MISS.
I SHUDDER TO THINK WHAT OUR BOARD OF GOVERNORS WOULD SAY ABOUT MY OWN BEHAVIOUR AS LEOPARD LILY! HA! HA!
The End

Fay's Best Friend

So —
THIS IS FUN!
YEAH! HEY, LOOK — THERE'S AMY AND KAREN FROM SCHOOL. LET'S JOIN THEM!
I'D RATHER NOT. IT'S NICER WITH JUST THE TWO OF US.
But, after a while —
THIS IS GREAT! RACE YOU ANOTHER LENGTH, SHELLEY.
NO, I'M FEELING A BIT COLD. I'M GOING OUT.
ARE YOU ALL RIGHT? I'LL GET OUT, TOO.
NO, I'M FINE, REALLY. THERE'S NO NEED.
AMY! KAREN! I'M GOING TO GET CHANGED NOW. CAN FAY SWIM WITH YOU?
OF COURSE!
BLOW!
Later —
WHY DID YOU SAY THAT? I HAD AN AWFUL JOB GETTING AWAY FROM THEM.
THEY WERE HAVING FUN. I THOUGHT YOU'D ENJOY YOURSELF.

IT WAS ALL RIGHT, BUT *YOU'RE* MY BEST FRIEND, SHELLEY. I ONLY REALLY WANT TO BE WITH YOU.

Back home —
MUM'S OUT. DO YOU WANT TO COME IN FOR A WHILE AND LISTEN TO RECORDS?
SURE! OH, LOOK! YOU'VE GOT NEW NEIGHBOURS.

SHE LOOKS NICE. LET'S SAY HELLO.
NO.
GREATEST HITS
But Shelley insisted —
AND THIS IS FAY. SHE LIVES NEXT DOOR. I BET YOU TWO WILL BECOME REALLY FRIENDLY.
I HOPE SO. I DON'T KNOW A SOUL ROUND HERE. I'M KIM, BY THE WAY.

PERHAPS I COULD CALL ROUND AND SEE YOU TOMORROW, FAY?
WELL . . . I . . . ER . . .
OF COURSE YOU CAN! FAY WOULD BE DELIGHTED.

16
WHAT DID YOU SAY THAT FOR? I'LL BE WITH *YOU* TOMORROW.
NO YOU WON'T. I'VE GOT SOMETHING ELSE ON, SO YOU CAN GET TO KNOW KIM INSTEAD.

Two days later —
HI! HOW DID IT GO WITH YOU AND KIM, THEN?
IT DIDN'T. I TOLD HER I WAS BUSY AND SHE SEEMED TO GET THE MESSAGE. I DON'T THINK SHE'LL BE ROUND AGAIN.

OH, FAY, HONESTLY!
WHAT? COME ON, LET'S GO SKATEBOARDING IN THE PARK.
THIS IS FUN!
YEAH. HEY — LOOK AT HIM!
WHAT ABOUT HIM?
HE'S GORGEOUS! AND HE'S SMILING AT YOU! I RECKON HE FANCIES YOU.
LET'S GO OVER!
NO! SHELLEY! I DON'T WANT . . .
OH! WHAT'S THE USE?
The three got talking —
THERE'S A GREAT FILM ON AT THE PICTURES THIS WEEK.
YEAH, FAY WAS SAYING THAT.
REALLY? PERHAPS YOU'D LIKE TO GO WITH ME?
UM . . . WELL, I . . .
SHE'D LOVE TO. SHE'S JUST A BIT SHY WITH BOYS.
GREAT! IT'S A DATE. I'LL MEET YOU AT HALF-PAST SIX OUTSIDE THE PICTURES.
SHE'LL BE THERE!

WHAT'S GOING ON, SHELLEY? YOU KNEW I DIDN'T WANT TO GO OUT WITH HIM BUT EVER SINCE YOU CAME BACK YOU'VE BEEN TRYING TO PERSUADE ME TO GO AROUND WITH OTHER PEOPLE. WHAT'S WRONG?
PERHAPS I'M JUST SICK OF YOU TAGGING AROUND AFTER ME *ALL* THE TIME.
THAT'S AN AWFUL THING TO SAY!
YOU ASKED FOR IT! STOP BEING SUCH A DRAG, FAY.
OH!
I CAN'T BELIEVE SHELLEY JUST SAID THAT! SHE'S SUPPOSED TO BE MY BEST FRIEND!
PERHAPS I *WILL* GO OUT WITH THAT BOY AFTER ALL. IT WOULD SERVE SHELLEY RIGHT!
But —
IT'S NO GOOD. I'M NOT ENJOYING MYSELF. HE'S NOT MY TYPE.
When the film was over —
THERE'S A DISCO ON THIS FRIDAY, FAY. I WAS WONDERING IF YOU'D LIKE TO GO TO IT?
I'D RATHER NOT, DAVE. THANKS FOR ASKING ME THOUGH. I'LL GET THE BUS HOME.
BUS STOP 18-21

WAS THAT YOUR BOYFRIEND?
NOT REALLY. HE ONLY LASTED ONE DATE.
DISCO
T·DAVI
THAT'S WHAT ALWAYS HAPPENS TO ME, TOO! I'M FED-UP WITH BOYS. I WISH I HAD A BEST FRIEND TO GO AROUND WITH INSTEAD, BUT I DON'T MAKE FRIENDS VERY EASILY.
NEITHER DO I.
WHY DON'T WE TEAM UP TOGETHER, THEN?
WELL . . . I . . .
I WAS GOING TO SAY I ALREADY HAVE A BEST FRIEND, BUT SHELLEY'S BEEN ACTING SO ODDLY LATELY, I'M NOT SURE IF I DO!
So —
OKAY!
LYDIA'S NICE. I'M SURE WE'LL GET ON REALLY WELL.
The next day —
I WONDER HOW FAY IS TODAY?

YOU'RE SO FUNNY, LYDIA! I'M GLAD WE'RE GOING AROUND TOGETHER.
OH! IT LOOKS LIKE SHE'S FOUND A NEW BEST FRIEND!
I KNOW I PUSHED HER INTO IT, BUT IT STILL HURTS TO SEE FAY ENJOYING HERSELF WITH SOMEONE ELSE. IT'S FOR THE BEST, THOUGH, BECAUSE IN A FEW DAYS' TIME SHE'LL FIND OUT THE TRUTH — THAT I DIED IN A CAR CRASH THREE DAYS INTO MY HOLIDAY, ALONG WITH MY PARENTS.
T WAS A REMOTE MOUNTAIN PASS. I NEW IT'D BE A WHILE BEFORE ANYONE OUND OUR BODIES, AND THAT GAVE E ENOUGH TIME TO COME BACK HERE AS A GHOST, TO FORCE FAY INTO MAKING NEW FRIENDS.
NOW SHE'S FRIENDS WITH LYDIA, SHE'LL FIND MY DEATH MUCH EASIER TO BEAR. BEFORE, WHEN SHE HAD NO-ONE ELSE, SHE'D HAVE BEEN DEVASTATED.
MY JOB IS DONE. THERE'S NO NEED FOR ME TO STAY ANY LONGER. GOODBYE, FAY. YOU WERE A GREAT BEST FRIEND . . .
The End

Having a ball at Dundee High!

Having

You *shall* go to the ball, Cinders — and you, too, Prince!

"Harry" strikes a pose!

Think putting on a musical play sounds fun? So did we! And, when we heard that Dundee High School was putting on a musical play of Cinderella, we couldn't resist popping along to the dress rehearsal and mixing with some of its stars!

THE production was Cinderella, and *Alison Young*, the first person we spoke to, had the starring role!

"I was desperate to be Cinderella as soon as we heard we were going to do it. I'm really enjoying doing this. My favourite part's in scene two where the ugly sisters get on at me for not having tea ready for them. It's also really funny seeing Richard (one of the ugly sisters) padding his bra backstage with socks!"

Cinderella's prince was *John Boyle*.

"It's great fun playing the prince. I really like my outfit. I've been a bit nervous today, though, with all the people. I'm glad I don't have to wear earrings and make-up like the ugly sisters."

Supporting the prince was Harry — the prince's trainer, a part not traditionally included in normal Cinderella productions — played by *Paul McMillan*.

"I wanted to be the prince at first but when our teacher said she wanted me to be Harry, I was quite happy. I thought it would be a good part. As his trainer, I'm a different kind of servant who helps him out."

Next, we met three people who certainly *didn't* mind dressing up — stepmother, *Stuart Coull*, and ugly sisters, *Richard Beaton* and *John Paul Bennett*.

Who put your make-up on, Stuart?

"Our teacher did my blusher and eyeshadow, but I did my own lipstick. I think my outfit's great! Originally I wanted to be an ugly sister, but I'm glad I was the stepmother. You get a

John Paul prepares to step out in style!

Hair we go! Richard adds the finishing touch!

A Ball!

Abracadabra! The fairy godmother shows her assistant how to tidy up!

Proud "Mum", Stuart, and sons . . . er, we mean daughters!

bit nervous, but you can't really see the audience because of the lights."

The ugly sisters, however, weren't nervous at all!

"It's loads of fun," said Richard. "I've always liked acting, but I prefer comical parts to straight roles. They're more of a laugh."

John Paul agreed. "It's great. At the auditions Richard and I had to pretend Cinderella was with us and be mean to her. No-one laughs at us in our costumes — they wouldn't dare!"

The simplest costume was worn by the fairy godmother's assistant, *Louise Gordon*, and consisted of a swimming costume and not much else!

"I'm freezing! I like the part, though. It's strange how it all ended up, because I wanted to be the fairy godmother and Victoria wanted to be Cinderella."

Instead, *Victoria Grant* won an equally glamorous role — that of the fairy godmother.

"I wanted to be Cinders, but I'm enjoying this. Acting's fun!"

So, did everything go all right on the night? You betcha! The production, written by Miles of Music, produced miles of smiles — from the cast and the audience!

Shall we dance? The grand finale!

DEBBIE CARTER was looking forward to Christmas. A week before the big day —
Christmas Wishes
HERE'S THE FAIRY FOR THE TOP OF THE TREE, MUM.
THAT OLD THING LOOKS REALLY TATTY. THROW IT AWAY, DEBBIE — I'LL BUY A NEW FAIRY IN TOWN TOMORROW.
NO! I LIKE THE OLD ONE. SHE'LL BE FINE FOR ONE MORE YEAR, MUM. HONESTLY!
WELL — IF YOU'RE SURE.
I AM! IT WOULDN'T BE CHRISTMAS WITHOUT OUR OLD FAIRY ON THE TOP OF THE TREE. THERE! SHE LOOKS PERFECT!

A few days later —
I SEE YOU'VE WRAPPED MRS HUNTER'S PRESENT. SHALL I TAKE IT ROUND TO HER HOUSE?
YES, PLEASE.
IT'LL BE ANOTHER LONELY CHRISTMAS FOR OUR NEIGHBOUR WITH HER ONLY NEPHEW AND HIS WIFE IN CANADA. HE PROMISED HER HE'D WRITE AND VISIT, BUT HE NEVER HAS.
POOR MRS HUNTER! I WISH HER NEPHEW WOULD VISIT HER. IT WOULD MAKE HER CHRISTMAS.
HELLO, MRS HUNTER!
COME IN, DEAR. I THOUGHT IT MIGHT BE MY NEPHEW, GEORGE. HE PROMISED TO COME BACK AND VISIT ME, YOU KNOW.
HE'S SURE TO ARRIVE SOON.
SHE'S BEEN SAYING THAT FOR TWO YEARS NOW. IT'S SO SAD.
THANK YOU FOR THE PRESENT, DEBBIE. STAY AND HAVE A CUP OF TEA.
OKAY. YOU SIT THERE, AND I'LL PUT ON THE KETTLE.

HAVE YOU FOUND EVERYTHING, DEBBIE?
YES. OH! THERE'S YOUR FRONT DOORBELL.
TEA
HI! IS AUNTIE ANNIE IN?
GEORGE!
MY DEAR BOY — HOW ARE YOU?
FINE, AUNTIE. I'VE COME FOR CHRISTMAS. I'M SORRY I HAVEN'T BEEN IN TOUCH BEFORE, BUT SETTING MYSELF UP IN CANADA TOOK ALL MY TIME.
BUT I'M A SUCCESS NOW! I'VE GOT A GOOD JOB AND A NICE HOUSE FOR ME AND PAT. WE WANT YOU TO COME BACK AND LIVE WITH US AFTER CHRISTMAS. WILL YOU DO THAT?
OH — I'D LOVE TO! IT'S MY WISH COME TRUE!
AND MINE! MRS HUNTER WILL HAVE A LOVELY CHRISTMAS NOW.

Later —
THERE'S GORGEOUS MARTIN POTTER. HE NEVER SEEMS TO NOTICE ME. I WISH HE'D ASK ME OUT.
HUH! HE HASN'T EVEN STOPPED TO CHAT.
The next afternoon —
HOW ARE YOUR CHRISTMAS FLOWER ARRANGEMENTS COMING ON, MUM?
I'VE RUN SHORT OF HOLLY, LOVE. WILL YOU GO TO THE COMMON AND CUT ME SOME MORE?
OKAY. OH! THERE'S CAROL COMING UP THE PATH. SHE LOOKS UPSET.
COME ON IN AND TELL ME WHAT'S WRONG.
MEMO
IT'S SPOT. THE DAFT PUP'S MISSING. I'M SURE HE'S GONE TO THE PARK. WILL YOU COME AND HELP ME LOOK FOR HIM?
OF COURSE! I'LL MEET YOU IN THE PARK AS SOON AS I'VE CUT SOME HOLLY FOR MUM AT THE COMMON.
THANKS. I'LL SEE YOU THERE.

Soon —
ONE MORE BRANCH SHOULD BE ENOUGH. CAROL'S SO WORRIED ABOUT SPOT. I WISH HE'D TURN UP SAFE AND SOUND.
Then —
OH! WHAT WAS THAT NOISE?
SPOT! KEEP STILL WHILE I UNTANGLE YOU FROM THE HOLLY.
THANK GOODNESS I'VE FOUND YOU! AND WHAT LUCK I CAME TO THE COMMON FIRST. CAROL WAS SURE YOU'D GONE TO THE PARK. WE MIGHT NEVER HAVE FOUND YOU.
The next few days passed quickly, and soon it was Christmas Day —
MERRY CHRISTMAS, DEBBIE!
WHAT AN ACE JUMPER! THANKS, MUM AND DAD.
I'VE HAD SOME SMASHING PRESENTS — CLOTHES, RECORDS, GAMES.
THERE'S ONE MORE FOR YOU HERE.
WHO'S IT FROM? I'M NOT EXPECTING ANY MORE.
YOU'D BETTER OPEN IT AND SEE.

M'MM! WHAT SUPER PERFUME!
AND THERE'S A NOTE INSIDE — OH! IT'S FROM MARTIN POTTER. HE SAYS HE'S TOO SHY TO ASK ME OUT TO MY FACE, BUT PLEASE WILL I GO TO THE DISCO WITH HIM ON NEW YEAR'S EVE?
CAN I?
I DON'T SEE WHY NOT.
I'LL TAKE ALL THE WRAPPING TO THE DUSTBIN.
AND I'D BETTER GET ON WITH THE DINNER.
IT'S BEEN A BRILLIANT CHRISTMAS. I MADE THREE WISHES — THAT MRS HUNTER'S NEPHEW WOULD VISIT HER, THAT MARTIN WOULD ASK ME OUT, AND THAT SPOT WOULD BE FOUND SAFE AND SOUND. AND THEY ALL CAME TRUE. I WONDER WHO GRANTED MY WISHES FOR ME?
The Granter of Wishes was very close at hand — right above Debbie's head, in fact.
It was the fairy's way of saying thank you, because Debbie had insisted she should be kept for one more year. So if your Christmas Fairy looks old and tatty, don't throw her away. You never know — you might be rewarded in an extra special way too!
THE END

BUNTY - A girl like you
NIGHTMARE ON SYCAMOR STRE
LET'S GO IN. I'VE HEARD IT'S REALLY SCARY.
A GOOD LAUGH MORE LIKE, JO.
THIS IS NOT THE SLIGHTEST BIT FRIGHTENING.
HUH! THAT WAS KIDS' STUFF!
Later, at the fair—
OOH! THIS'LL BE SCARY.
GHOST TRA
WHAT A PAIR OF WIMPS.
OKAY, IF YOU'RE SO BRAVE, WHY DON'T YOU GO IN BY YOURSELF? JO AND I WILL TAKE THE FIRST CAR.
OKAY BY ME, LISA.
WOW! THAT WAS REALLY TERRIFYING. HOPE BUNTY'S ALL RIGHT.
HERE SHE COMES, NOW.
WELL, BUNTY? HOW WAS IT?
NOT SCARY AT ALL . . .
. . . I DON'T KNOW WHAT ALL THE FUSS WAS ABOUT!

MARIE'S MAGIC WHISTLE
KIND-HEARTED Marie Baxter lived on a housing estate in London—
HI, MRS O'CONNOR. ARE YOU GOING TO THE SHOPS? I'LL WALK WITH YOU AND CARRY YOUR BAG, IF YOU LIKE.
THAT'S VERY KIND OF YOU, DEAR. THANK YOU.
Mrs O'Connor lived alone next door to Marie.
THAT DOG ALWAYS GIVES ME A FRIGHT. IT'S SO NOISY.
IT'S HARMLESS, MRS O'CONNOR.
YOU DID THAT ON PURPOSE!
I DID NOT!
THE BRYANT TWINS ARE ALWAYS SQUABBLING THESE DAYS!
IT'S PROBABLY JUST A PHASE, MRS O'CONNOR.
In town—
GREENGROCER
CHEMIST
I'M GOING TO BUY SOME FRUIT AND VEGETABLES.
I NEED SOME SHAMPOO. I'LL MEET YOU BACK HERE IN HALF AN HOUR AND CARRY YOUR SHOPPING HOME FOR YOU.
YOU'RE WASTING YOUR MONEY! IT'LL TAKE MORE THAN *THAT* TO IMPROVE *YOUR* STRAGGLY HAIR, MARIE BAXTER!
WHY DOES SONIA ALWAYS HAVE TO BE SO HORRIBLE?

MORE THAN THAT! IT'S A VERY SPECIAL WHISTLE. MY GRANDFATHER GAVE IT TO ME WHEN I WAS A LITTLE GIRL IN IRELAND. HE GOT IT FROM HIS GRANDFATHER AND ORIGINALLY IT BELONGED TO A LEPRECHAUN. I'VE NO FAMILY TO PASS IT ON TO, SO I'D LIKE *YOU* TO HAVE IT, DEAR.

THANKS, MRS O'CONNOR.

IT'S AS THOUGH THE WHISTLE'S PLAYING ITSELF! MRS O'CONNOR SAID IT WAS SPECIAL — AND SHE WAS RIGHT!
TEE..DEE...

And—
I ENJOYED THAT! NOW LET'S WATCH THE FOOTBALL.
NO, NO, WE'LL WATCH THE NEWS.
MUM AND DAD WERE REALLY GRUMPY BEFORE I STARTED PLAYING. BUT NOW THEY'RE HAPPY. I WONDER JUST HOW SPECIAL THIS TIN WHISTLE IS?

Next day, Marie decided to find out—
THERE'S THE SMITHS' DOG BARKING AS USUAL. NOW LET'S SEE WHAT THIS WHISTLE CAN DO.

TEE..DUNN.TEE DO
JUST AS I THOUGHT — IT'S STOPPED BARKING!

And—
THE BRYANT TWINS ARE FIGHTING EACH OTHER AS USUAL!
IT'S MINE!
NO, IT ISN'T — IT'S MINE!

But, as soon as Marie played her whistle—
YOU HAVE IT FIRST, THEN I'LL HAVE A GO.
YEAH — WE'LL SHARE IT.
TEE. DEE..

WHEN PEOPLE AND ANIMALS HEAR IT, THEY BECOME HAPPY AND NICER! MAYBE IT REALLY *DID* BELONG TO A LEPRECHAUN. MAYBE IT'S MAGIC!

At school—

RIGHT, CLASS, GET YOUR BOOKS OUT.

MR BROWN LOOKS BORED STIFF, AS USUAL!

I WONDER IF MY WHISTLE CAN HELP? I'LL JUST PLAY A FEW NOTES.

And, a minute later—

CHEER UP, YOU LOT! WE'RE ABOUT TO START READING A MARVELLOUS NEW PLAY.

IT WORKED! MR BROWN'S SUDDENLY FULL OF ENTHUSIASM!

Over the next few days Marie noticed that the effects of the whistle lasted only a few minutes—

I'M SORRY, IT WAS MY FAULT.

DON'T MENTION IT. ACCIDENTS HAPPEN.

STILL, WHILE IT *DOES* LAST, THE WORLD'S A FAR NICER PLACE!

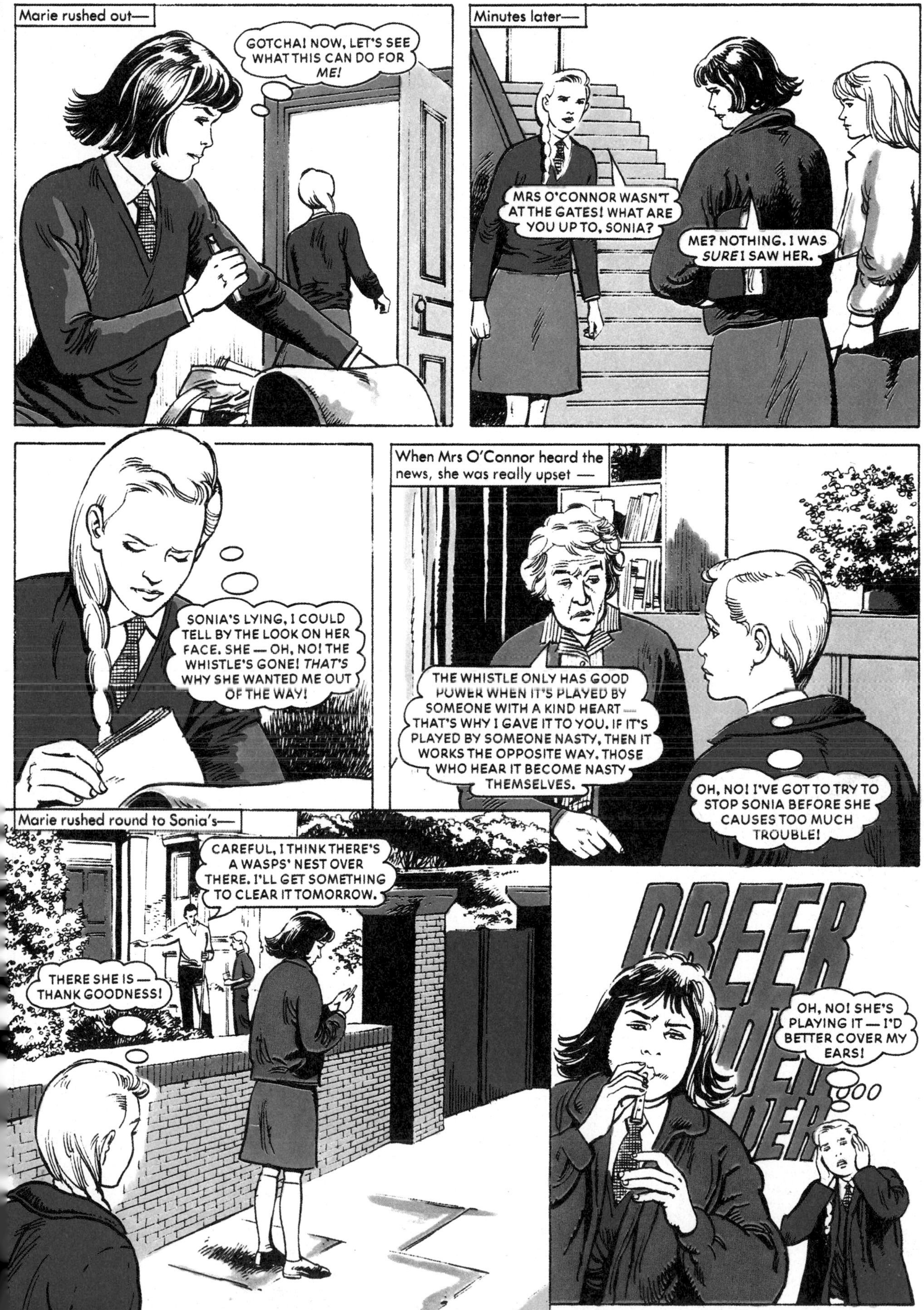

Marie rushed out—

GOTCHA! NOW, LET'S SEE WHAT THIS CAN DO FOR *ME!*

Minutes later—

MRS O'CONNOR WASN'T AT THE GATES! WHAT ARE YOU UP TO, SONIA?

ME? NOTHING. I WAS *SURE* I SAW HER.

SONIA'S LYING, I COULD TELL BY THE LOOK ON HER FACE. SHE — OH, NO! THE WHISTLE'S GONE! *THAT'S* WHY SHE WANTED ME OUT OF THE WAY!

When Mrs O'Connor heard the news, she was really upset —

THE WHISTLE ONLY HAS GOOD POWER WHEN IT'S PLAYED BY SOMEONE WITH A KIND HEART — THAT'S WHY I GAVE IT TO YOU. IF IT'S PLAYED BY SOMEONE NASTY, THEN IT WORKS THE OPPOSITE WAY. THOSE WHO HEAR IT BECOME NASTY THEMSELVES.

OH, NO! I'VE GOT TO TRY TO STOP SONIA BEFORE SHE CAUSES TOO MUCH TROUBLE!

Marie rushed round to Sonia's—

CAREFUL, I THINK THERE'S A WASPS' NEST OVER THERE. I'LL GET SOMETHING TO CLEAR IT TOMORROW.

THERE SHE IS — THANK GOODNESS!

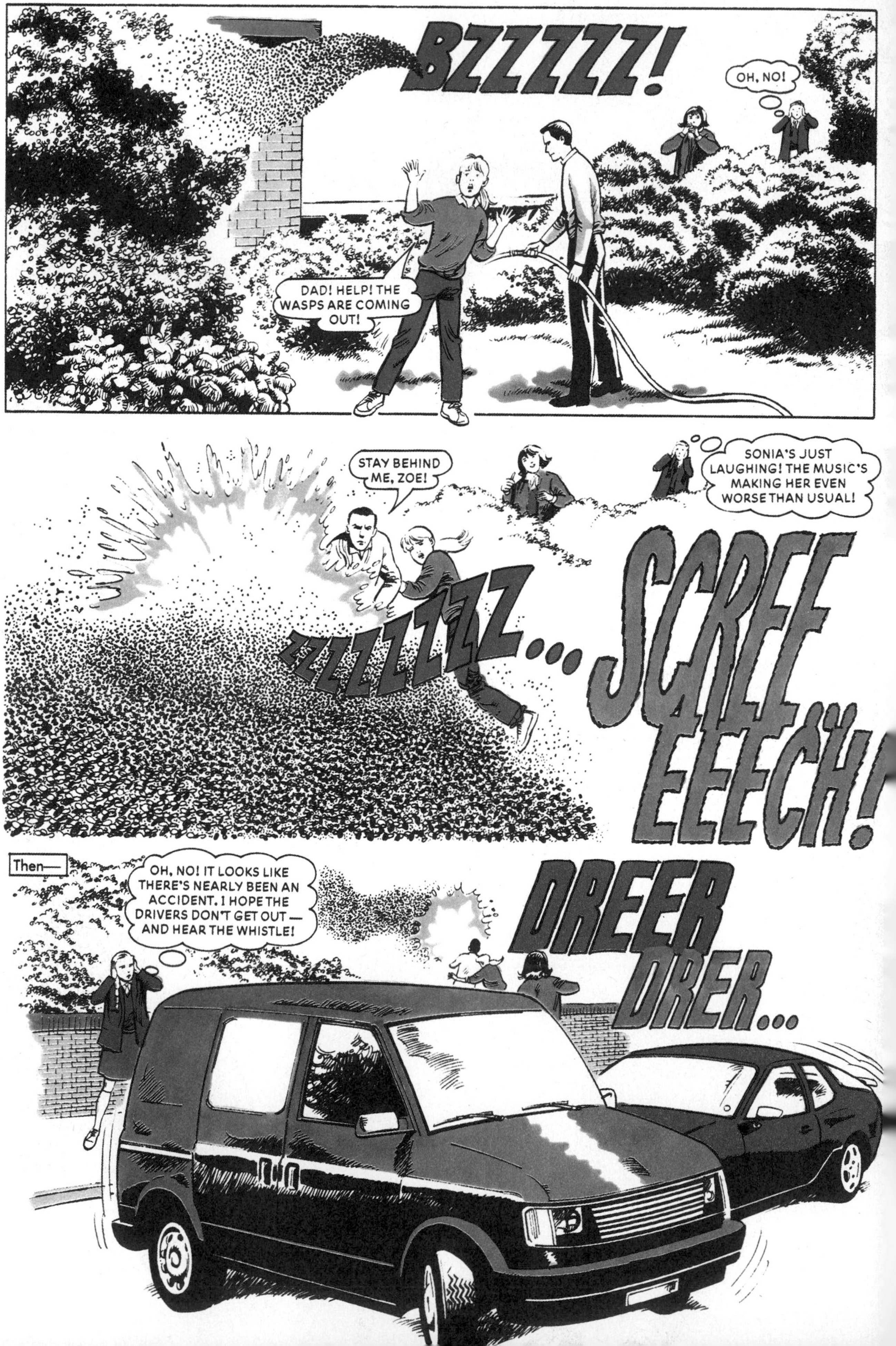

BZZZZZ!
OH, NO!
DAD! HELP! THE WASPS ARE COMING OUT!

STAY BEHIND ME, ZOE!
SONIA'S JUST LAUGHING! THE MUSIC'S MAKING HER EVEN WORSE THAN USUAL!
ZZZZZZZZ... SCREEEEECH!

But—
YOU OUGHT TO WATCH WHERE YOU'RE GOING!
ME? WATCH IT YOURSELF!
I SUPPOSE THE BAD EFFECTS FROM THE WHISTLE WILL ONLY LAST A FEW MINUTES, TOO — BUT THAT COULD BE LONG ENOUGH FOR SOMETHING AWFUL TO HAPPEN!

I CAN'T TALK TO SONIA, BUT I'VE GOT TO DO *SOMETHING!* WAIT A MINUTE, I'VE JUST HAD AN IDEA. I'VE GOT TO FOLLOW HER.

DREER.. DREER..
I'M SICK OF BEING GOALIE!
NEITHER OF YOU CAN *KICK* THAT BALL!

SAYS WHO? TRY AND CATCH *THAT* THEN!
THAT'S THE *LAST* THING I INTEND TO DO!

Marie moved, and—
OOF!
SHE'S DROPPED THE WHISTLE — GREAT!

THIS IS EXACTLY WHAT I HOPED WOULD HAPPEN!

TWEETLE... DEE....
As soon as Marie started playing—
THE WASPS ARE GOING —THANK GOODNESS!
SORRY, DID I HURT YOU? I'LL GET MY MUM.
And—
NO HARM DONE, THEN?
NONE AT ALL!
THERE COULD HAVE BEEN, THOUGH — VERY EASILY! I'M TAKING THE WHISTLE HOME AND PUTTING IT IN A SAFE PLACE.
I'LL KEEP IT LOCKED AWAY — LIKE MRS O'CONNOR DID — AND ONLY PLAY IT ON SPECIAL OCCASIONS! THEN I CAN PASS IT ON TO MY CHILDREN!
AFTER ALL, MAGIC'S TOO MAGIC TO USE EVERY DAY! I'M SURE MRS O'CONNOR AGREES!
THE END

HAGGIS

I LOVE A RUN IN THE CAR.

OH, NO!

I DIDN'T REALISE...

...IT WAS GOING TO BE A DRIVING LESSON!
L

DOG SHOW

JAB
PULL
LIFT
PROD

BITE

SENT OFF!

HUH, HOW DEGRADING.

HOW CAN FIFI LOWER HERSELF LIKE THAT?

ER - MAYBE THERE'S ENOUGH LEFT FOR TWO?

The Four Marys

MARY FIELD, Mary Cotter, Mary Radleigh and Mary Simpson were in the Third Form at St Elmo's School for Girls, and were the best of friends. One afternoon —

The following afternoon—
TEAS ARE BEING SERVED NOW, MUM. DO YOU HAVE TIME . . .
WE'D LOVE TO, MARY, BUT IF WE DON'T GET THE NEXT BUS TO THE STATION, WE'LL MISS OUR TRAIN HOME.
WE'LL SEE YOU AGAIN SOON.
'BYE! SAFE JOURNEY!
EVERYONE ELSE IS STILL BUSY. I MIGHT GO BACK TO OUR STUDY, AND READ . . .
HI, THERE.
OH, HI!
I'M CLIVE, WHAT'S YOUR NAME?
MARY. MARY SIMPSON. I TAKE IT YOU'VE GOT A SISTER HERE?
SSH! NOT SO LOUD. IT'S MY SISTER AND HER PAL I'M DODGING. I GOT TIRED OF BEING DRAGGED ROUND THE SCHOOL BY THOSE TWO.
I DON'T SUPPOSE . . . IF YOU'RE FREE, YOU'D LIKE TO SHOW ME ROUND THE GROUNDS?
WHY NOT?
Later—
CLIVE'S NICE. HE'S EASY TO TALK TO.
I HOPE ST BARTOPH'S HAS PLAYING FIELDS LIKE THESE. I'M STARTING THERE NEXT WEEK, YOU SEE.
CLIVE!

MABEL, THE DISGRACE! YOUR BROTHER IS TALKING TO SIMPSON.
GOODNESS! HE'S MABEL'S BROTHER!
MUMMY AND DADDY ARE WAITING FOR US IN THE TEA TENT, CLIVE.

'BYE, MARY! I'LL SEE YOU!
WELL, THAT EXPLAINS WHY HE WAS TRYING TO DODGE HIS SISTER!

YOU SPENT THE AFTERNOON WITH MABEL'S BROTHER?
HE'S NOTHING LIKE MABEL, FIELDY. HE'S GOOD FUN!
THEN YOU'RE RIGHT. HE'S *NOTHING* LIKE MABEL!

Simpy thought no more of it. Then, the next week—
I'VE JUST HAD A PHONE CALL FROM CLIVE, AT ST BARTOPH'S — HE'S INVITED ME OUT TO TEA, THIS AFTERNOON!
GOOD FOR YOU, SIMPY!
WHAT? HE CAN'T HAVE!

TSK! YOUR BROTHER DATING A COMMON SCHOLARSHIP GIRL — IT'S SHAMEFUL, MABEL!
I GET THE FEELING VERONICA'S JUST A TEENY BIT JEALOUS, GIRLS.

After that, Clive and Simpy saw each other regularly, on half-days and at weekends —

MARY SIMPSON'S BRAGGING THAT CLIVE'S TAKING HER TO THE CINEMA, MABEL.
THIS CAN'T GO ON, VERONICA. IT'S UP TO US TO PUT A STOP TO IT — AND I KNOW HOW! WE'LL PAY CLIVE A VISIT.

OF COURSE, CLIVE, YOU DO REALISE THAT MARY SIMPSON TELLS HER SILLY FRIENDS EVERYTHING ABOUT YOUR DATES?
OH, REALLY?
IT UPSETS US TO HAVE TO TELL YOU, CLIVE, BUT WE DON'T LIKE TO HEAR THEM MAKING FUN OF YOU . . .

OH, I'LL SUFFER IT.
MARY'S NEVER SAID AS MUCH, BUT I KNOW THAT MABEL AND VERONICA CAN'T STAND HER AND HER FRIENDS!
BUT, CLIVE — HER PEOPLE ARE ONLY COMMON . . .

OUR DAD'S "ONLY" A BUILDER, MABEL — EXCEPT THAT HE'S MADE A LOT OF MONEY OUT OF IT.
HOW CAN YOU COMPARE OUR FATHER TO . . . TO . . . WELL, REALLY!

WELL, IF WE CAN'T PUT CLIVE OFF SIMPSON, WE'LL PUT HER OFF HIM!
CLIVE'S HAD ANOTHER LONG LETTER FROM JEANETTE, HIS GIRLFRIEND BACK HOME. HE MISSES HER SO, VERONICA — HE WRITES TO HER EVERY DAY.

DID YOU HEAR THAT, SIMPY?
DON'T WORRY, COTTY. CLIVE TOLD ME ABOUT JEANETTE. SHE WAS HIS GIRLFRIEND — FOR THREE WEEKS, LAST YEAR. HE HASN'T SEEN OR HEARD FROM HER IN MONTHS!
DRAT! SHE KNOWS!

Next day—
I'LL MEET YOU AT THREE TOMORROW AFTERNOON, IN ELMBURY TOWN SQUARE. SEE YOU THEN, CLIVE.
THIS IS OUR CHANCE, VERONICA.
Dear Mary Sorry, but I can't make it until four o'clock. See you then - Clive
THIS WILL DO THE TRICK.
YOU, FIRST FORM KID! TAKE THIS TO MARY SIMPSON IN THE THIRD FORM. TELL HER A BOY GAVE IT TO YOU. WE'RE, ER — PLAYING A JOKE ON HER. HERE'S FIFTY PENCE FOR YOU!
NOW SHE WON'T TURN UP TILL FOUR. CLIVE WILL THINK HE'S BEEN STOOD UP.
THAT'LL BE THE END OF MARY SIMPSON! BRILLIANT, MABEL!
AND I'LL GO ALONG AT JUST AFTER THREE — TO COMFORT HIM!
THIS IS A NOTE FROM CLIVE, TO SAY DON'T TURN UP TILL FOUR. FUNNY — WHY DIDN'T HE RING? HE ALWAYS DOES.
CAN I SEE THAT, SIMPY?
WHO DO WE KNOW WHO HAS A PEN WITH THIS SHADE OF PURPLY INK?
MABEL, THAT'S WHO! IT'S A SNOBS' TRICK!
HOW SILLY CAN THEY GET?

TEN PAST THREE. CLIVE WILL BE THINKING SHE'S NOT COMING — *OH!* SHE — SHE'S *HERE!*
Later—
DID YOU HAVE A GOOD TIME, SIMPY?
YES — BUT I'VE GOT SOMETHING TO TELL YOU. CLIVE AND I HAVE FINISHED.
WHAT? YOU HAVEN'T LET THOSE SNOBS GET TO YOU, SIMPY?
IT'S NOT THAT, COTTY. I JUST DIDN'T FEEL READY TO GO STEADY YET. AND WE'VE GOT A LOT ON, IN SCHOOL TOO, AT THE MOMENT — SO I TOLD CLIVE I WANTED TO FINISH. WE'LL STILL BE FRIENDS, THOUGH.
WHAT?
THAT COMMON CREATURE HAS DITCHED MY BROTHER — OF ALL THE NERVE!
GREAT! NOW HE'S ALL MINE! I'VE FANCIED CLIVE FOR AGES.
Veronica didn't hang about!
CLIVE, I WAS WONDERING . . . IF YOU'RE AT A LOOSE END NOW, YOU COULD ALWAYS TAKE *ME* OUT. ANY TIME!
ER — NO, THANK YOU. I'VE DECIDED TO GIVE UP DATING, AND CONCENTRATE ON MY SCHOOLWORK. I'VE A LOT TO CATCH UP WITH! 'BYE, VERONICA.
Back at St Elmo's—
THIS IS ALL MARY SIMPSON'S FAULT! SHE'S PUT CLIVE OFF GIRLS ALTOGETHER!
YOU KNOW, I WONDER IF I COULD EVER DO ANYTHING TO PLEASE THOSE SNOBS?
UNLIKELY, SIMPY — BUT I SHOULDN'T LET IT WORRY YOU! HA! HA!
THE END

TREE MENDOUS!

We've a bumper batch of puzzles for you around this special Christmas tree!

A

```
     C B
    R E S N
    L T V I
   L A U P E Y
  S R C R M U R C
  T A H K L I I A
 O N L R E K C A R C
T D E T I Y U E F D A T
L I S F S A T N A S R I
E N S E I T R A P L E O N L
S V I C R G M R H G I E L S O W
K R O P T A E D T O Y S E V
E O T E L T S I M B A U B L E S
     N Y
     D O
    N E J W
    U E X N
    F R P V
```

C

B

Hidden in this tree — reading backwards, forwards, up, down and diagonally — you'll find these thirty Christmas words: baubles, bells, candles, cards, carols, Christmas, cracker, disco, eat, eve, fairy, fun, gift, ice, joy, kiss, love, mistletoe, Noel, parties, presents, reindeer, Santa, sleigh, snow, star, tinsel, toys, turkey, yule. Search 'em out!

GET CRACKING

Dotted around the page you'll find four Christmas crackers marked A, B, C and D. Which two are identical?

YUM!

Help Bugsy through this maze to his Christmas dinner!

D

MAGIC!

Fill in the missing numbers to make each column — across, diagonally and up and down — add up to the same total in this magic square!

3	2	?
0	2	4
?	2	1

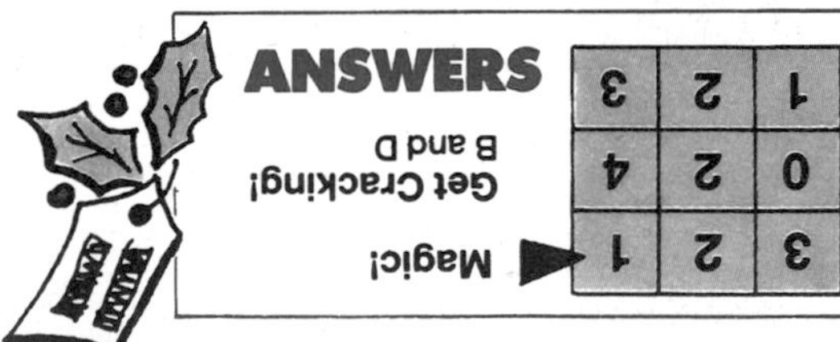

ANSWERS

Magic!

3	2	1
0	2	4
3	2	1

Get Cracking! B and D

IT'S CHRISTMAS

How many words of three letters or more can you make from the word CHRISTMAS?

0-20 *FAIR*   21-30 *GOOD*   31+ *EXCELLENT*

A Family Heirloom

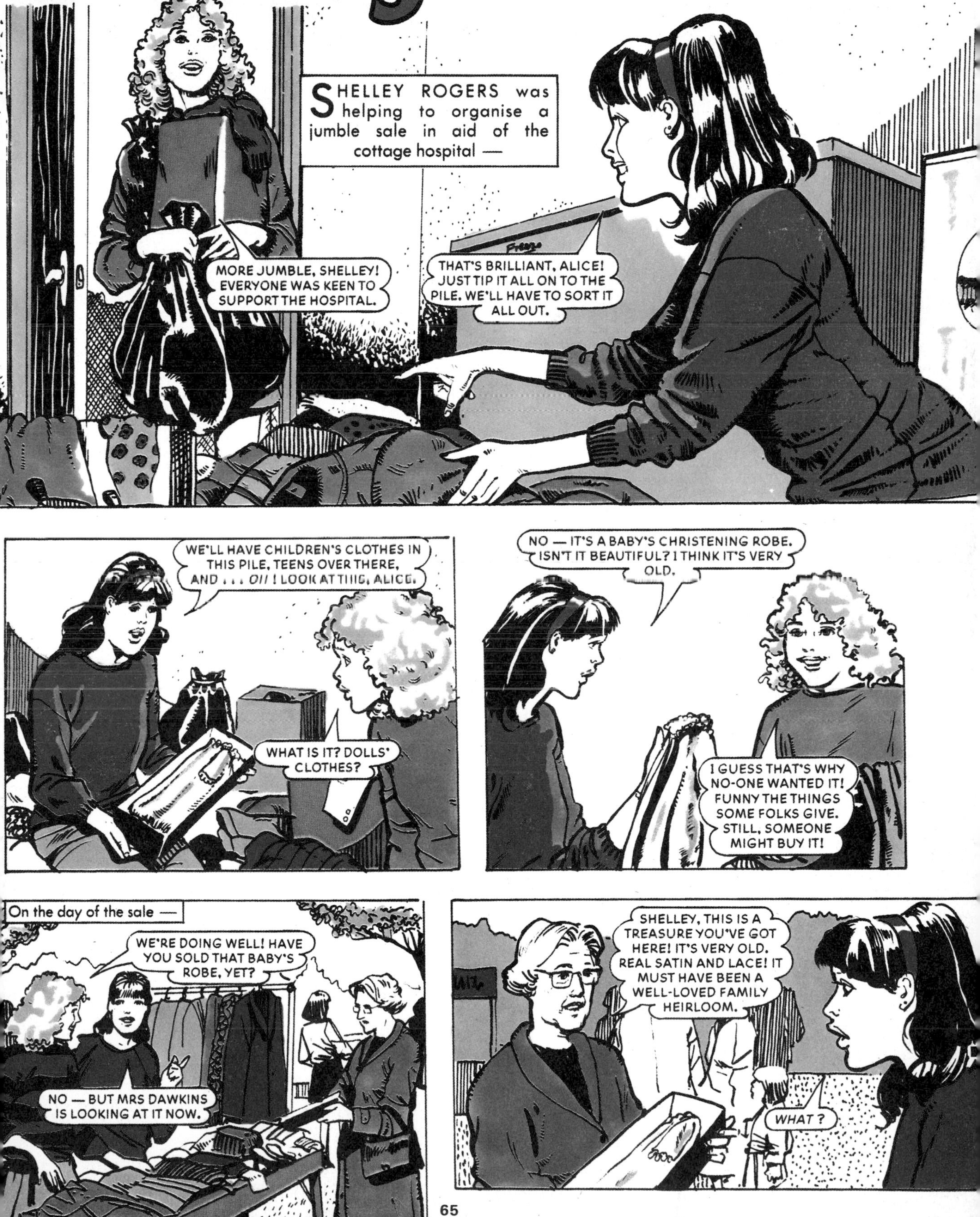

SHELLEY ROGERS was helping to organise a jumble sale in aid of the cottage hospital —

MORE JUMBLE, SHELLEY! EVERYONE WAS KEEN TO SUPPORT THE HOSPITAL.

THAT'S BRILLIANT, ALICE! JUST TIP IT ALL ON TO THE PILE. WE'LL HAVE TO SORT IT ALL OUT.

I'M SURPRISED THE OWNER PARTED WITH IT. WELL — IT'S MY LITTLE GRANDDAUGHTER'S CHRISTENING SOON, SO I'LL GIVE YOU FIVE POUNDS FOR IT!
ER — NO! NO, THANK YOU. IT'S NOT FOR SALE!
EH?

TURNING DOWN A FIVER? SHELLEY, ARE YOU MAD?
IT'S WHAT MRS DAWKINS SAID — A FAMILY HEIRLOOM. WHAT IF THIS GOT INTO THE JUMBLE BY MISTAKE?

I'D FEEL TERRIBLE IF WE SOLD IT, AND SOMEONE *DID* WANT IT BACK. I'LL PUT IT ASIDE FOR NOW.

Next day —
Dolls' House Museum
MISS HETTISHAM WHO RUNS THE LITTLE DOLLS' HOUSE MUSEUM COLLECTS OLD COSTUMES. PERHAPS THIS CAME FROM HER.

NO, DEAR, IT'S NOT FROM MY COLLECTION. I'D NEVER LOSE AN ANTIQUE AS PRECIOUS AS THIS. I'D SAY IT'S FROM THE EIGHTEEN-EIGHTIES. IT'S BEEN LOVINGLY KEPT, IT'S IN EXCELLENT CONDITION, AND WORTH QUITE A BIT.
WELL, THAT SETTLES IT. IT MUST HAVE GOT INTO THE SALE BY ACCIDENT. I'LL TRY TO FIND THE OWNER, BUT WHERE DO I START LOOKING?

At Alice's house —
NO, I DON'T REMEMBER WHICH BAG IT CAME OUT OF, SHELLEY. IT COULD'VE BEEN ANY OF THEM. WE COLLECTED STUFF FROM ALL OVER TOWN.
THEN WE'LL HAVE TO TRY TO WORK IT OUT. *WHO* MIGHT OWN A VICTORIAN CHRISTENING ROBE? PROBABLY SOME WEALTHY FAMILY.

MRS BRENLEY-SMYTHE FROM THE LARCHES GAVE US A WHOLE LOAD OF THINGS. THEY'RE THE WEALTHIEST FOLK AROUND HERE.
GOOD THINKING, ALICE. I'LL CHECK IT OUT!

But —
NO, DEAR, IT DIDN'T COME FROM US. MY WORD, ISN'T IT BEAUTIFUL?

WELL, NO LUCK THERE! WHERE NEXT? HEY, I KNOW!

I CAN'T SAY I RECOGNISE IT, MY DEAR, BUT THEN I CHRISTEN SO MANY BABIES, AND THEY ALL WEAR ROBES!
OH, WELL. IT WAS A GOOD IDEA.

HAVE YOU PUT AN ADVERTISEMENT IN THE LOST AND FOUND SECTION OF THE LOCAL PAPER?
NO, BUT I'LL GIVE IT A TRY. THANK YOU, REVEREND WILSON!

And so —
FILL IN CARD
IT WILL COST THREE POUNDS FIFTY.
OH! I HAVEN'T GOT THAT MUCH. I'M SORRY.

SO MUCH FOR ADVERTS. HANG ON! I COULD PUT A CARD IN THE NEWSAGENT'S WINDOW. I'LL WRITE "FOUND — VICTORIAN CHRISTENING ROBE" AND GIVE MY PHONE NUMBER! THAT WON'T COST MUCH.
NEWSAGEN

In the shop —
. . . WE WERE SO TERRIBLY SAD TO LOSE IT.

OH, YOU MUST HAVE BEEN. YOU POOR THING.
IT WAS IN OUR FAMILY OVER A HUNDRED YEARS, YOU KNOW.
OH !

EXCUSE ME! ARE YOU TALKING ABOUT A BABY'S CHRISTENING ROBE? ONLY, I'VE FOUND . . .
NO! ABOUT A VALUABLE VASE MY CLEANING LADY BROKE. AND DON'T INTERRUPT!
REALLY !

BOTHER. I THOUGHT I'D STRUCK LUCKY THAT TIME.
PLEASE WOULD YOU DISPLAY THIS CARD IN —
HANG ON, LOVE — DID YOU SAY A BABY'S ROBE?

ONLY, MY NEIGHBOUR'S DAUGHTER HAS LOST SOMETHING THAT'S BEEN IN HER HUSBAND'S FAMILY FOR YEARS. I THINK IT MIGHT HAVE BEEN BABY CLOTHES.
PLEASE, CAN YOU GIVE ME THE ADDRESS?

Shelley went straight round —
THIS IS THE PLACE.

EXCUSE ME — DID YOU GIVE SOME JUMBLE TO THE HOSPITAL SALE? ONLY —
OH! WHERE DID YOU GET THAT? IT LOOKS LIKE THE BOX OUR ROBE WAS IN!

THIS ROBE?
OH! THANK GOODNESS! I THOUGHT I'D NEVER SEE IT AGAIN! I DIDN'T KNOW HOW I WAS GOING TO TELL MY IN-LAWS! PLEASE COME IN.

IT'S OUR JASON'S CHRISTENING SOON, AND I'D HAD THE ROBE OUT, TO AIR. I MUST HAVE SCOOPED IT UP WITH THE JUMBLE. I CAN'T THANK YOU ENOUGH, LOVE! YOU WILL COME TO THE CHRISTENING, WON'T YOU?
YES, PLEASE! I'D LOVE TO!

And —
I THOUGHT THE ROBE WAS BEAUTIFUL WHEN I FIRST SAW IT, BUT ON LITTLE JASON, IT'S PERFECT!
THE END

Sarah's Songbird
IN the year 1880, the doctor was a regular visitor to the Faversham household. A weak and sickly child, Sarah Faversham had lost the use of her legs, after contracting infantile paralysis.
SHE HAS EATEN VERY LITTLE AGAIN TODAY, DOCTOR.
YOU ARE VERY PALE, MY DEAR. DO YOU TAKE MUCH FRESH AIR?
IN SUMMER, PAPA WHEELS MY CHAIR AROUND THE GARDEN EVERY DAY, DOCTOR.
I THINK PERHAPS YOU SHOULD SIT OUTSIDE FOR AN HOUR OR SO EACH DAY, SARAH. FRESH AIR WILL GIVE YOU AN APPETITE, AND BRING SOME COLOUR TO THOSE CHEEKS!
BUT WILL SHE NOT CATCH COLD? SINCE SHE CANNOT MOVE AROUND, WE MUST BE MOST CAREFUL THAT SHE DOES NOT CATCH A CHILL . . .
But the doctor insisted —
THIS IS MOST STRANGE — I AM USED TO SITTING INDOORS. I FEAR THAT MAMA MAY BE RIGHT, AND THAT I SHALL CATCH COLD. I SHALL RING MY LITTLE HAND-BELL, FOR PAPA TO TAKE ME INSIDE.
RIGHT, LET'S GET YOU INDOORS.
OH! PAPA, WAIT! WHAT IS THAT SONG I HEAR?
IT'S A LITTLE ROBIN WHO SINGS TO ME. PAPA, I THINK HE IS HUNGRY. MAY I GIVE HIM SOME BREAD?

SEE, HE IS TAKING THE CRUMBS! HOW CLOSE TO ME HE COMES — HE IS NOT AFRAID OF ME!
NOW HE IS THANKING YOU FOR HIS DINNER!
SUCH A SWEET SONG. OH, PAPA — MAY I STAY OUTSIDE AND LISTEN?
Later —
SARAH, YOUR CHEEKS ARE FLUSHED AND YOUR EYES ARE SHINING! HAVE YOU CAUGHT A CHILL?
OH, MAMA — I FED A LITTLE ROBIN, AND HE SANG TO ME! MAY I TAKE SOME BREAD OUT FOR HIM AGAIN TOMORROW?
HE MAY NOT BE THERE, DEAR.
But he was there the next day, and the next —
HELLO, MY LITTLE FRIEND — YOU ARE WAITING FOR ME! YOU SEEM TO KNOW THE EXACT TIME I WILL COME!
Then, one day —
WHY, SARAH — HE EATS FROM YOUR HAND!
THIS IS THE FIRST TIME HE HAS DONE SO, PAPA. I HOPED HE WOULD — HE HAS BECOME SO VERY TAME!
Spring passed into summer, and Sarah spent longer and longer outside —
SUCH A CHANGE IN MY LITTLE PATIENT! SHE IS NOT SO THIN NOW, NOR SO PALE.
IT IS A JOY TO HEAR HER LAUGHTER, DOCTOR!

Then, one day in the late autumn —
NO, SARAH, YOU MUST NOT GO OUT TODAY. IT IS VERY COLD.
BUT, MAMA, WHEN IT IS COLD, MY ROBIN NEEDS ME EVEN MORE! I SHALL ONLY STAY OUT LONG ENOUGH TO FEED HIM.
But, the next day —
ATISHOO! ATISHOO!
SARAH! YOU HAVE CAUGHT A COLD! OH, I BLAME MYSELF. I SHOULD NEVER HAVE LET YOU OUT. YOU MUST GET TO BED IMMEDIATELY!
I'M SURE IT IS ONLY A SLIGHT CHILL, MY DEAR. SHE WILL SOON BE WELL.
IT IS A WARNING. THE DAYS ARE NOW TOO COLD FOR HER TO SIT OUTSIDE. SARAH SHALL NOT GO OUT AGAIN UNTIL THE SPRING!
NO, MAMA! PLEASE . . .
Sarah's chill passed, but she was not allowed outside again.
PAPA PUTS OUT FOOD EVERY DAY, BUT MY ROBIN DOES NOT COME. HE WILL TAKE FOOD FROM NO-ONE BUT ME. HOW SILENT THE GARDEN IS WITHOUT HIS SINGING.
The early snow fell —
WILL YOU NOT EAT A LITTLE OF YOUR BROTH, DEAR? IT WILL DO YOU GOOD.
I AM NOT HUNGRY, MAMA.
Over the following weeks, Sarah grew steadily weaker —
COME, CHILD. JUST ONE MORE MOUTHFUL . . .
COLD — SO COLD — WHY DOES HE NOT COME?

Finally —
SHE WILL TAKE NO FOOD OR DRINK, DOCTOR. SHE HAS NOT MOVED OR SPOKEN FOR DAYS . . .
MRS FAVERSHAM, I — I CAN DO NO MORE TO HELP SARAH. I AM AFRAID SHE IS SLIPPING AWAY FROM US.
Suddenly, Mr Faversham opened the window —
WILLIAM! HAVE YOU GONE MAD? THE DRAUGHT WILL SURELY KILL OUR LITTLE GIRL!
NO, MY DEAR! LISTEN. DO YOU NOT HEAR IT? LISTEN, SARAH! *LISTEN!*
SHE — SHE IS OPENING HER EYES!
UPON MY SOUL!
MY . . . ROBIN . . . I HEAR HIM . . . I HEAR MY ROBIN SINGING!
MY ROBIN! YOU ARE ALIVE — YOU HAVE COME BACK TO ME!
And from that moment, Sarah's recovery began. Before long —
JUST LOOK AT HER! IT IS A MIRACLE, MRS FAVERSHAM — A MIRACLE!
YOU CAME BACK WHEN I NEEDED YOU MOST, MY LITTLE ROBIN. NOW MAMA SAYS I MAY COME EVERY DAY TO FEED YOU. WE SHALL BOTH GROW STRONG TOGETHER.
The End

Christmas KEEP-FIT!

If you tend to put on pounds at Christmas, let Bugsy come to your rescue with this cracking keep-fit guide!

* Build up your arm muscles fighting for (and pulling) the last Christmas cracker.

*** Search the house from top to bottom for hidden pressies!**

* Race your brother or sister to the advent calendar each day!

*** Take your dog on long walks to show off his new Christmas collar and lead.**

* Ambush your enemies with snowballs . . .

*** . . . then *run!***

* Exercise your tongue licking stamps . . .

*** . . . and your hands sticking them!**

* Devise a great dance routine for the disco!

*** Put all your sporty new presents to use immediately.**

* Stir the Christmas pud for Mum!

*** *Walk* (or stagger?) home after buying all your presents.**

*** Start exercising your elbows for the January Sales!**

* Chase handsome hunks with some mistletoe . . .

*** . . . and run off when wimps draw near.**

* Offer to take out all the rubbish on Christmas morning.

*** Do step aerobics as you pin up decorations!**

* S-t-r-e-t-c-h to decorate the top of the tree!

*** Try learning to ski or skate! Scrambling to your feet all the time will work that body!**

* Fight your sister to see who gets to read your Bunty Annual first.

*** Stomp up and down when you're carol singing to keep warm.**

* Better still, offer to do the collecting.

* Deliver all your Christmas cards by hand — even the ones to Scotland!

* Flex your muscles pulling the wishbone at Christmas dinner!

*** Ban the remote control for your TV. You'll have to get up from your seat to change channels.**

SALLY DIXON was looking forward to the school holidays —
IT'S NOT FAIR! WE'RE AT SCHOOL ALL DAY, AND THEN THEY GIVE US HOMEWORK AS WELL! I CAN'T WAIT FOR THE HOLIDAYS! I NEED THE REST.
I WOULDN'T MIND A BREAK, TOO. NO CHANCE OF THAT THOUGH WITH YOU, DAD, STEVIE AND FRANCES TO LOOK AFTER.
Mum For A Week
OH, COME ON, MUM! IT'S NOT AS IF YOU GO OUT TO WORK OR ANYTHING. LIFE'S ONE LONG HOLIDAY FOR YOU.
THAT'S WHAT YOU THINK! I'LL HAVE YOU KNOW THIS IS A BIG HOUSE TO KEEP CLEAN, FRANCES IS A VERY DEMANDING TODDLER AND WHAT WITH EVERYBODY'S LIKES AND DISLIKES — COOKING FOR FIVE IS A NIGHTMARE!
BUT HOUSEWORK'S A DODDLE!
ALL RIGHT. IF YOU THINK THAT — YOU DO IT!
I CAN'T. I HAVE TO GO TO SCHOOL.
I DIDN'T MEAN NOW. I MEANT IN THE HOLIDAYS. THE UNIVERSITY IS RUNNING A THREE WEEK CRASH COURSE IN LOCAL HISTORY. I'D LOVE TO SIGN ON, BUT I CAN'T BECAUSE OF FRANCES AND THE HOUSE.
ONLY THREE WEEKS TO LEARN OUR LOCAL HISTORY? THIS AREA HAS BEEN INHABITED SINCE ROMAN TIMES. YOU'LL NEVER LEARN IT ALL IN THREE WEEKS!
OF COURSE I WILL. BUT I WON'T GET THE CHANCE UNLESS YOU'LL DO THE HOUSEWORK FOR ME. BUT IF IT'S TOO MUCH, YOU ONLY HAVE TO SAY SO.

OF COURSE IT'S NOT TOO MUCH. I'LL RUN THE HOUSE. IT'LL BE SIMPLE!
GREAT! THANKS. AND I'LL BECOME A STUDENT AGAIN. IT'LL BE A WONDERFUL CHANCE FOR ME TO REALX.

RELAX? WHEN YOU'RE A STUDENT? BOY, MUM DOES HAVE A SHOCK COMING TO HER!

On the first day of the holidays —
I'M OFF, THEN. SURE YOU CAN COPE?
OF COURSE! GOOD LUCK WITH YOUR LESSONS.
STEVIE'S WATCHING TV, AND FRANCES HASN'T WOKEN UP YET. I CAN LIE IN AND READ MY MAG.

But —
JUICE! SALLY! JUICE!
SOUNDS LIKE FRANCES *HAS* WOKEN UP NOW. OH, WELL.

THERE YOU ARE, NICE ORANGE. YOU DRINK THAT AND I'LL FIND YOU SOME CLOTHES TO WEAR.

But —
FRANCES! STOP TIPPING YOUR DRINK ON YOUR BED.
TEDDY WANT JUICE TOO.

TEDDIES DON'T DRINK JUICE.
EVERYTHING'S SOAKING. I'LL HAVE TO STRIP THE BED.

THERE — YOU CAN WEAR YOUR BLUE DRESS TODAY.
NO! NO LIKE BLUE DRESS!

WAAH! WAAH!
ALL RIGHT. YOU CHOOSE WHAT YOU WANT TO WEAR.

STEVIE! STOP FLICKING YOUR CORN FLAKES ON THE FLOOR.
THEY'RE NOT CORN FLAKES. THEY'RE SUPER MINI HAND GRENADES. BOOM! FIRE!
MY BROTHER AND SISTER ARE DRIVING ME MAD. THEIR GAMES ALWAYS SEEMED A LAUGH WHEN I DIDN'T HAVE TO CLEAR UP AFTERWARDS.

But, at last —
PHEW! AUNTIE KATH HAS TAKEN FRANCES OFF MY HANDS FOR A FEW HOURS, AND STEVIE'S GONE OUT TO PLAY! PEACE AT LAST!

I'VE PUT THE WASHING IN. NOW TO PLAN TONIGHT'S SUPPER MENU. I KNOW! STEAK AND CHIPS!

But —
THERE ARE ONLY TWO PIECES OF STEAK IN THE FREEZER. THAT'S OUT. MAYBE I'LL DO FRIED FISH AND POTATOES INSTEAD.

BUT NOT FOR STEVIE. HE DOESN'T LIKE FISH. I'LL HAVE TO FRY HIM A BURGER. OH — AND CHIPS TOO, BECAUSE HE'S NOT KEEN ON POTATOES EITHER. THEN WE'LL HAVE PEAS, AND I'LL DO BAKED BEANS FOR FRANCES. IT'S THE ONLY VEG SHE'LL EAT.

WAIT A MINUTE! FISH, BURGER, POTATOES, CHIPS, PEAS AND BAKED BEANS. I'LL NEED SIX DIFFERENT RINGS TO COOK THAT — AND WE ONLY HAVE FOUR. I KNOW! I'LL DO A PIE AND CHICKEN NUGGETS FOR FRANCES BECAUSE SHE WON'T EAT PASTRY.

But —
THAT WON'T WORK EITHER, BECAUSE PIES NEED TO BE COOKED AT 180° AND THE NUGGETS AT 220°. IT'S IMPOSSIBLE! WHY CAN'T THEY ALL EAT THE SAME?
The Recipe Book

Then —
HEY, WHAT'S THAT SPLASHING NOISE?

OH, NO! THE WASHING MACHINE HAS PACKED UP. AND THE KITCHEN FLOOR'S SOAKED.

YES, IT IS AN EMERGENCY.
IT TOOK ME AN HOUR TO CLEAN THE KITCHEN FLOOR AND NOW IT'S TAKING ME AGES TO FIND AN ENGINEER WHO'S FREE.

Eventually —
THIS WAY, MR BLEWITT.

Then —
HI, SALLY. I'VE BROUGHT FRANCES BACK.
ALREADY? I HAVEN'T EVEN SAT DOWN YET.

That evening —
NICE MEAL, SALLY. THANK YOU.
I HOPE THEY REALISE THE PLANNING THAT WENT INTO IT.
GLAD YOU LIKED IT. CAN SOMEBODY HELP ME WITH THE WASHING UP?

But —
DAD AND I ARE GOING TO THE FOOTBALL. SEE YOU.
AND I HAVE HOMEWORK TO DO. SORRY, SALLY.
BLOW! I CAN'T REALLY COMPLAIN THOUGH. THAT'S THE EXCUSE I USUALLY USE.

A few days later —
CLEANING, DUSTING, PREPARING MEALS, WASHING UP, LOOKING AFTER FRANCES, THERE'S NO END TO IT! I WAS WRONG. THIS IS HARD WORK. I WISH I COULD GIVE IT UP AND ENJOY THE REST OF MY HOLIDAY. BUT I CAN'T LET MUM DOWN NOW.

Then —
NOW THERE'S SOMEONE AT THE DOOR. IF IT'S ANOTHER DOUBLE GLAZING SALESMAN, I'LL SCREAM! WE'VE ALREADY HAD THREE ROUND THIS WEEK.

But —
MUM!
SORRY. I FORGOT MY KEY.

YOU'RE EARLY. I SUPPOSE YOU WERE GIVEN THE AFTERNOON OFF. HUH! THAT'LL CONVINCE YOU EVEN MORE THAT STUDENTS HAVE AN EASY TIME. BUT WE DON'T HAVE AFTERNOONS OFF AT MY SCHOOL.
NO. I HAVEN'T BEEN GIVEN THE AFTERNOON OFF. I'VE LEFT.
WHAT?

I WAS WRONG. BEING A STUDENT WASN'T SO MUCH FUN AS I REMEMBERED. STUDYING'S HARD WORK AND I HATED BEING TOLD WHAT TO DO THE WHOLE TIME. I'M USED TO BEING MY OWN BOSS AT HOME.
BOSS AND WHOLE ARMY OF WORKERS, I'D SAY. HOUSEWORK'S HARD GOING!

SO YOU DIDN'T ENJOY YOURSELF EITHER? NEVER MIND! GIVE ME THAT PINNY. I'LL FINISH UP HERE.
AND I'LL TAKE YOUR BOOKS BACK TO THE LIBRARY. WE'LL BOTH GO BACK TO HOW WE WERE!

NO MORE HOUSEWORK OR BABY-MINDING FOR ME! HEY — I WONDER IF SOMEONE WILL INVENT A ROBOT TO DO THE CHORES? I HOPE SO!
THE END

LUV, LISA XX
ONLY A FEW DAYS TO CHRISTMAS — IT'S REALLY EXCITING!
Martin's always up to something!
HEY, LISA. LET'S SEE IF WE CAN FIND WHERE MUM AND DAD HAVE HIDDEN OUR PRESSIES.
BUT, MARTIN. SURELY YOU KNOW THAT SANTA BRINGS OUR PRESSIES ON CHRISTMAS EVE?
OH, YEAH, SURE. BUT WHAT ABOUT THE OTHER ONES — THE ONES THAT MUM AND DAD BUY!

I couldn't resist it!
COME ON. MUM AND DAD'S BEDROOM. BET THEY'RE HIDDEN IN HERE.
But —
NOPE. NOTHING UNDER HERE. OH, I GIVE UP.
HUH, TYPICAL GIRL. THERE'S STILL MILLIONS OF PLACES TO LOOK.
HEY! I'VE GOT IT. THE AIRING CUPBOARD!
NOT BAD, SIS. LET'S GO.
But —
FOUND ANYTHING?
NOPE. THEY'VE REALLY GOT ME THIS YEAR. BUT THERE'S ONE MORE PLACE . . .
So, it was out to the garage.
IT'S LOCKED!
OH, WELL. LET'S GO IN. IT'S *FREEZING*!

Martin wasn't giving up!
COME ON, WHILE DAD'S WATCHING TV WE CAN GET THE KEY TO THE GARAGE. HE KEEPS IT ON HIS BEDSIDE CABINET.
OH, ALL RIGHT.
ANYONE COMING?
NO — HURRY UP!
Rumbled!
OKAY, WHAT ARE YOU TWO UP TO?
MUM! OH. WE WERE . . . ERM . . .
JUST GOING TO TIDY YOUR BEDROOM. NICE SURPRISE FOR YOU.
REALLY? WELL IN THAT CASE, LISA, YOU CAN HOOVER AND YOU CAN DO THE DUSTING, MARTIN. THANKS, KIDS.
GREAT!
So —
NICE ONE, MARTIN. NOW WE HAVE TO DO HOUSEWORK — AND THE GARAGE KEYS AREN'T EVEN THERE.
DAD MUST HAVE THEM IN HIS POCKET, THEN.

THERE'S HIS JACKET. I'LL HAVE A QUICK LOOK.
Then —
HANGING DAD'S JACKET UP FOR HIM, MARTIN?
ER — YEAH.
JUST THOUGHT I'D HELP KEEP THE PLACE TIDY, MUM.
TELL YOU WHAT, I'LL DO THAT. IF YOU TWO ARE IN SUCH A HELPFUL MOOD, YOU CAN PUT THIS IRONING AWAY FOR ME.
NOT DOING VERY WELL, ARE WE?
WELL, IF YOU'RE GOING TO COMPLAIN ALL THE TIME I THINK WE SHOULD JUST FORGET IT.
Later —
I BELIEVE YOU TWO ARE IN A TIDYING-UP MOOD. HOW WOULD YOU LIKE TO CLEAN UP IN THE GARAGE?
OKAY, DAD.

NOW WE'LL BE ABLE TO FIND THE PRESSIES.
YEAH!
But —
I'M FED-UP, I'M FREEZING AND I'M EXHAUSTED! REMIND ME NEVER TO LISTEN TO YOUR BRIGHT IDEAS IN FUTURE.
I DON'T UNDERSTAND IT. THEY'VE GOT TO BE HERE. WE'VE LOOKED EVERYWHERE ELSE.
YORK
6600
On Christmas Day —
THANKS FOR THE PRESENTS, MUM AND DAD. ER — JUST AS A MATTER OF INTEREST — WHERE DID YOU HIDE THEM THIS YEAR?
HA! WE KNEW WHAT YOU TWO WERE UP TO ALL ALONG, SO WE HID THEM WHERE WE KNEW YOU'D NEVER LOOK . . .
. . . AMONGST ALL THE RUBBISH UNDER YOUR OWN BEDS! HA-HA!
Huh! Well they won't get away with that one next year!
See you in Bunty every week!
Luv, Lisa.
P.S. Merry Christmas!

BUGSY and FR
HI, GIRLS! MEET THE GANG. THEY'RE ALL TOTALLY LOVABUGGLE!
CAPTAIN BUGSEYE
RAMBUG
BUG ROGERS
KYLIE BUGOGUE

NDS
'BUGGLES
JUNE BUGGY
BILLY THE BUG
BUGSY MALONE
TEA BUG
BUGGY HOLLY

Stars of

If you've ever wanted to know wha
goes on behind the scenes when we
shoot a photo-story, listen up
We're about to reveal all —
with a little help from
the stars of St K's

When you're shooting a photo-story, there are so many things that can go wrong, you can never be over-prepared! If the weather's not the same two days running, you could have to re-do shots you'd already taken. If you don't pay attention to continuity, someone could be wearing a green jumper in one picture and a sweatshirt or cardi in the next!

But, shooting Sara At St K's and Summer at St K's, which appeared last year in your weekly "Bunty" and in the Summer Special, *none* of these things happened! Everyone double-checked what they were wearing and carrying for each picture, so even though all the shots were taken out of sequence, when we came to put the stories together, all the shots that were supposed to run on from each other actually did! Phew!

Location shots outside the school, which is in St Andrews, proved a bit more difficult! It took over an hour in the photographer's car and the school minibus to find a bus stop 'in the country'. However, there were perks, too! Using a real sweetshop meant its owner rewarded our four heroines with free sweets!

Extras were actually real teachers, cooks and groundsmen from St Katharines School, with only one Bunty member of staff putting in an appearance as the ski resort receptionist!

Working with animals is always supposed to be difficult, but with lots of digestive biscuits and the help of Mr and Mrs Bayley, who run the school, their dogs, Glen and Fiddich, did almost everything we asked!

In order not to disrupt the school too much (shooting six weekly episodes plus the Summer Special story took us 3½ days) night shots had to be done during the day, with curtains closed, and any telltale clocks hidden from view!

Tricky shots involving lots of pupils and extra teachers — such as the swimming, hockey and fire-fighting scenes — took longer to organise and were left till last.

Shooting Sara At St K's and Summer At St K's was interesting, exhausting, and *fun*! We all enjoyed producing them and hope you all enjoyed reading them!

No expense spared! A fire scene means a real fire, and real . . . cough . . . smoke!

Beware low-flying photographers!

St K's!

Facts "N" Figures

- ★ Each photograph had to be taken three or four times to make sure we had a perfect shot of each scene — with no-one blinking, giggling or making funny faces in the background!
- ★ The summer special story (four pages) used up four rolls of film — 144 photographs!
- ★ We started work at 9.30 am and finished around 6 pm — for 3 days! The fourth day we took about an hour!
- ★ The weekly serial (twenty-four pages in all) used eighteen rolls of film — 648 photographs!
- ★ Everyone said their lines every time we took a photograph, so they were all word-perfect by the end of each shot.
- ★ Numerous cups of tea and pieces of shortbread were consumed in the process!

Lots of it, too!

All change! Day becomes night!

A rare chance to relax between shots!

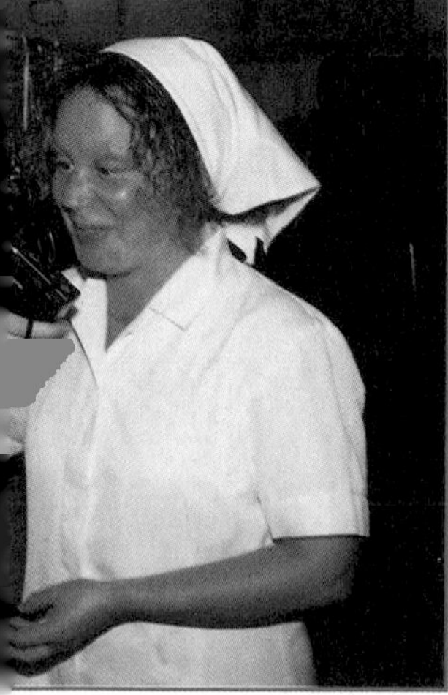

When being photographed, it's important not to pull faces . . .

. . . or laugh at the wrong time!

Somewhere in the bushes lurks a pupil with biscuits!

Accidents *can* happen. Beth hurt her arm during filming and had to miss a few scenes.

Front Page News

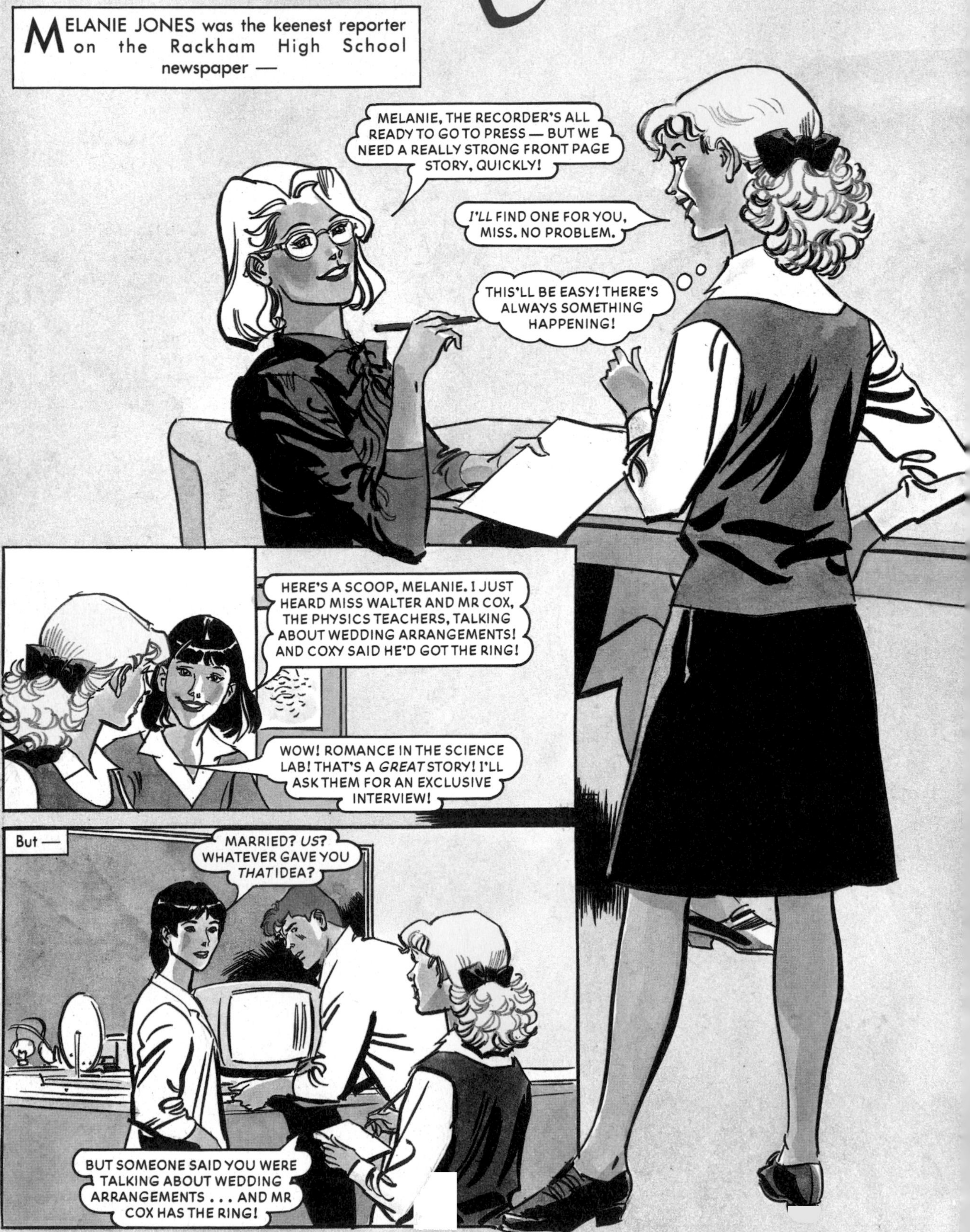

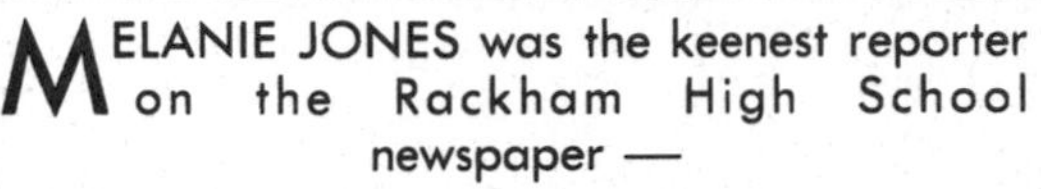

MELANIE, THE RECORDER'S ALL READY TO GO TO PRESS — BUT WE NEED A REALLY STRONG FRONT PAGE STORY, QUICKLY!

I'LL FIND ONE FOR YOU, MISS. NO PROBLEM.

THIS'LL BE EASY! THERE'S ALWAYS SOMETHING HAPPENING!

HERE'S A SCOOP, MELANIE. I JUST HEARD MISS WALTER AND MR COX, THE PHYSICS TEACHERS, TALKING ABOUT WEDDING ARRANGEMENTS! AND COXY SAID HE'D GOT THE RING!

WOW! ROMANCE IN THE SCIENCE LAB! THAT'S A *GREAT* STORY! I'LL ASK THEM FOR AN EXCLUSIVE INTERVIEW!

But —

MARRIED? *US*? WHATEVER GAVE YOU *THAT* IDEA?

BUT SOMEONE SAID YOU WERE TALKING ABOUT WEDDING ARRANGEMENTS . . . AND MR COX HAS THE RING!

IF YOU MUST KNOW, THE ARRANGEMENTS ARE FOR THE WEDDING OF A MUTUAL FRIEND OF OURS!
AND I'VE GOT THE RING, BECAUSE I'M GOING TO BE THE BEST MAN!
OH! S-SORRY!
Later —
HUH! "SCIENCE TEACHERS GO TO FRIEND'S WEDDING" ISN'T MUCH OF A FRONT PAGE STORY! HEY, *THAT* COULD BE THOUGH! DONNY JACKSON — THE POP STAR — IS HERE!
DONNY JACKSON LIVE IN RACKHAM
DONNY'S GIVING A CONCERT TONIGHT, BUT I DON'T HAVE A TICKET. I'LL WAIT HERE AND INTERVIEW HIM WHEN HE COMES OUT.
DONNY JACKSON
STAGE DOOR →
But —
HERE HE COMES! HELP — I'M BEING TRAMPLED!
STAGE DOOR →
DONN-EEE!
DONN-EEE!
OH, NO — HE'S BEING DRIVEN OFF IN THAT LIMO! AND ALL I SAW WAS THE BACK OF HIS HEAD!
SO MUCH FOR ME INTERVIEWING DONNY JACKSON. I'M *NEVER* GOING TO GET A REALLY GOOD STORY BY TOMORROW.
IT'S A SHAME ABOUT THIS PARK CLOSING . . .
EXCUSE ME! I'M A REPORTER. DID YOU SAY THIS PARK WAS BEING CLOSED DOWN?
WELL, MY MARVIN WORKS DOWN AT THE TOWN HALL, AND HE'S HEARD THAT THEY'RE GOING TO BUILD A FACTORY HERE!

THEY CAN'T CLOSE OUR PARK DOWN! I'VE GOT TO GET TO THE TOWN HALL AND GET ALL THE FACTS! THIS'LL MAKE AN ACE STORY . . .
MAY I SEE THE MAYOR, PLEASE? IT'S IMPORTANT — I'M FROM THE RACKHAM RECORDER!
HE'S IN A MEETING. YOU'LL HAVE TO WAIT.
So Melanie waited — and waited!
IT'LL BE A REAL SCOOP FOR THE RECORDER IF WE BREAK THE NEWS ABOUT THE PARK FIRST! OH, WHY'S HE TAKING SO LONG?
Finally —
MR MAYOR, I REPRESENT THE RACKHAM RECORDER. CAN YOU TELL ME THE TRUTH ABOUT THE PARK BEING SOLD OFF AS A FACTORY SITE?
EH? WHAT?
AH, YES, THAT IDEA. SOMEONE BROUGHT IT UP AT THE LAST COUNCIL MEETING, BUT WE THREW IT OUT AT ONCE.
OH — I SEE.
WHAT A WASTE OF TIME! I'M GLAD ABOUT THE PARK, BUT I STILL HAVEN'T GOT A STORY. IT'S HOPELESS. I'M NEVER GOING TO FIND ONE IN TIME, NOW . . .
MEEOWW!
OH, YOU POOR LITTLE THING — YOU'RE STUCK! IT'S OKAY, PUSS, I'LL SOON HAVE YOU DOWN!
MEEOWW!

RIGHT, DOWN YOU — *EEEEK!* I DIDN'T REALISE IT WAS SO HIGH UP HERE!
I — I'M SO S-SCARED I C-CAN'T MOVE! NOW *I'M* STUCK! *HELP!*
Shortly —
IT'S ALL RIGHT, LOVE — STAY THERE! THE FIRE BRIGADE'S ON ITS WAY!
S-STAY HERE? WHERE DOES HE THINK I'M *GOING*?
And soon —
OH, NO! THERE'S STEVEN FROM SCHOOL TAKING A PHOTOGRAPH! HOW EMBARRASSING!
Next day —
WELL DONE, MELANIE! YOU CERTAINLY GOT US A FIRST-CLASS FRONT PAGE STORY!
YES, MISS . . .
RACKHAM RECORDER
SCHOOL PUPIL IN DRAMATIC RESCUE
SCOOP REPORTER SCOOPED FROM TREE
THOUGH I WASN'T PLANNING ON *STARRING* IN IT! OH, WELL . . . IT *DID* MAKE A GOOD STORY! I SUPPOSE . . .
THE END

LISA'S DIARY

MONDAY

School was totally *boring* today. Debbie fell in love (again)! This time it's Mickey Smith from the fifth form. She thinks he already has a girlfriend, though. Becky came round to help me give Daisy a bath. What a disaster! We ended up wetter than the dog — might as well have got in with her. Martin is sucking up to Mum and Dad because he wants a new mountain bike for Christmas. It's got about a million gears!

TUESDAY

Oops! Daisy's got dandruff. Dad says we can't have rinsed the doggy shampoo off properly. Debs was fed-up today because she saw Mickey holding hands with his girlfriend. I went round to Jackie's with Daisy tonight. Jackie's still mad-keen on her keyboard playing. I just wish she didn't play it so loud! Daisy spent the whole night hiding under the settee. I felt like joining her sometimes. Jackie *has* improved, though. Maybe one day she'll be in a famous band. You never know.

WEDNESDAY

I've just finished a *mountain* of homework. Honestly, you go to school all day and then do homework all night! Becky phoned tonight. We decided to go out at the weekend to the Mega-Bowl so I'll have to save my cash and see if I can get an advance on next week's pocket money from Dad. Hope he's in a good mood! I found out that Mum and Dad are buying Martin the mountain bike for Christmas! Heard them speaking about it in the kitchen while they did the dishes. Just as well the shop's keeping it for them until Christmas Eve — they couldn't exactly hide it under a bed! Wonder what they're getting me?

THURSDAY

I'll have to think about *my* Christmas shopping. Think I'll get Martin some smart gloves for riding his bike. Don't know about Mum, Dad and Ali, though. Debs and Jackie are coming to the Mega-Bowl too. Hope I'm better at it than I was the last time — I hardly knocked down any pins. Had my favourite for tea tonight — spicy chicken and stir-fried vegetables. Yum! Next door's cat was in again. I think it likes our house better than its own.

FRIDAY

It was really exciting at school today! Debbie got a note from a secret admirer! We spent all day (well, between classes) trying to work out whose hand-writing it was. She's hoping it's from Mickey Smith, but somehow I don't think so. Dad gave me a whole fiver when he came home from work — and treated us all to an Indian carry-out. It was great. Can't wait till tomorrow!

SATURDAY

Debbie, Jackie and Becky came round for me and Mum gave us a lift to the bowling. And guess who was there? Mickey Smith and his girlfriend! Debbie nearly fainted. Then Nerdy Nigel from the third form turned up with all his horrible mates, and it turned out it was *him* who'd sent the note to Debbie. None of us could bowl straight for laughing (well, that's my excuse). They hadn't seen us when they came in and one of them was talking about Nigel writing love letters to Debs! I was glad Debs saw the funny side of it too. Just when I thought I was never going to get the hang of it I scored a strike. Everyone cheered like mad and I got really embarrassed. It was a great day, though. Hope we go back soon.

SUNDAY

Took Daisy to the park and did my paper round, then watched TV all afternoon. Mum and Dad were asking what I would like for Christmas. I thought about a typewriter. It might be really handy. I decided to get *everyone* gloves for Christmas — Martin cycling gloves, Dad gardening gloves, Mum suede gloves and Ali woolly gloves. Brilliant! That's my Christmas shopping list worked out!

Gifts Gifts
PAY HERE
Bunty – A Girl Like You
HAVEN'T YOU FINISHED YOUR CHRISTMAS SHOPPING YET, BUNTY? THIS IS TORTURE!
I KNOW, LISA, BUT I'VE STILL TO BUY DAD'S PRESENT.
OW! MY TOES!
COME ON — THIS DEPARTMENT STORE HAS A CAFE. LET'S GRAB A COKE.
I'LL BE GLAD WHEN CHRISTMAS IS OVER. I COULDN'T GO THROUGH ALL THIS AGAIN.
NEVER MIND — THAT'S OUR SHOPPING DONE.
OH, NO! I'VE FORGOTTEN MUM'S PRESENT. I'LL HAVE TO GO BACK IN THERE!
THAT'S IT FINALLY OVER. CHRISTMAS DAY TOMORROW — YIPPEE!
On Boxing Day —
DID YOU HAVE A GOOD CHRISTMAS, BUNTY?
BRILLIANT, JO! I GOT EVERYTHING I WANTED.
WHAT ARE WE GOING TO DO NOW?
I KNOW, LISA — LET'S GO SHOPPING.
SHOPPING? BUT, BUNTY, WE'VE JUST FINISHED SHOPPING FOR CHRISTMAS AND IT WAS SHEER TORTURE!
I KNOW, BUT THE SALES START TODAY — WE MIGHT GET SOME GREAT BARGAINS!
SALE
SALE

MABEL AND VERONICA

—THE THIRD FORM SNOBS

MABEL LENTHAM and Veronica Laverly were the worst enemies of the Four Marys at St Elmo's School for Girls.
One day, Mabel had a dental appointment —

HOT BUTTERED MUFFINS, CAKES, AND TEA FOR TWO, PLEASE.
OH, NO! HERE COME THE MARYS.
OVER HERE, WAITRESS!
YOU'LL HAVE TO WAIT. I'M SERVING THESE GIRLS AT THE MOMENT.
THOSE FOUR ARE SO RUDE. THEY LOWER THE TONE OF THE WHOLE SCHOOL.
SERVED AT LAST! HERE'S YOUR COFFEE, COTTY.
SUGAR?
NO! YOU KNOW I DON'T TAKE IT. I'M SWEET ENOUGH ALREADY!
CAREFUL!
NOW LOOK — THERE'S SUGAR ALL OVER THE FLOOR.
LET'S THROW IT AT THE SNOBS!
THAT'S ENOUGH!
OW! STOP IT!

FIRST YOU'RE RUDE, THEN YOU ATTACK THE OTHER CUSTOMERS. GET OUT! YOU'RE BANNED.
A GOOD THING TOO!

Next day —
MISS MITCHELL HAS MARKED THE PROJECTS YOU DID. WHAT ARE THE RESULTS, HEADMISTRESS?
COTTY WORKED REALLY HARD ON HERS. SHE DESERVES TO WIN.

But —
THE TOP MARK OF 86 WINS FIRST PRIZE FOR — MABEL LENTHAM!
WELL DONE, MABEL!

VERONICA WAS A CLOSE SECOND WITH 84. MOST OF THE CLASS GOT OVER 60 — EXCEPT THE FOUR MARYS, WHO FAILED TO GET EVEN HALF MARKS.
TUT! TUT! YOU FOUR MUST TRY HARDER. YOU SPEND TOO MUCH TIME SOLVING MYSTERIES, AND NOT ENOUGH WORKING.

MABEL'S PRIZEWINNING PROJECT WILL BE DISPLAYED ON FOUNDER'S DAY FOR ALL THE SCHOOL TO SEE.
NOT IF I CAN HELP IT!
INK

THERE!
SIMPSON! WHAT A SPITEFUL THING TO DO! GO AND STAND IN THE CORNER FOR THE REST OF THE LESSON.

I'M ASHAMED OF YOU, MARY SIMPSON.
I'M GLAD PEOPLE ARE FINDING OUT HOW AWFUL THOSE MARYS REALLY ARE. I'M FED-UP WITH THE WAY THEY ALWAYS GET THE PRAISE AT THIS SCHOOL.
A few days later —
HOW'S YOUR ENTRY FOR THE THIRD FORM ART COMPETITION COMING ON, MABEL?
QUITE WELL. I'M OFF TO HOCKEY PRACTICE NOW. I'M PLAYING FOR OUR HOUSE IN THE HOCKEY CUP FINAL.
GOOD WORK, MABEL! YOU SHOULD DO WELL IN THE MATCH TOMORROW.
Sure enough —
COME ON, BEE'S HOUSE!
MABEL'S GOT THE BALL. SURELY FIELDY CAN STOP HER SCORING.
NO! THAT'S HER THIRD.
A HAT-TRICK! WELL DONE, MABEL!

WAIT A MINUTE! WHAT DO YOU FOUR LOOK LIKE?

WE DECIDED TO JAZZ UP OUR UNIFORM, MISS CREEF!

IT — IT'S A DISGRACE!

OH, COME ON, CREEFY! WHERE'S YOUR SENSE OF FASHION?

HOW DARE YOU CALL ME BY THAT NAME? YOU FOUR WILL NOT GO TO THE PRIZE-GIVING CEREMONY. YOU CAN COLLECT LITTER IN THE SCHOOL GROUNDS.

HA! HA! LOOK AT THOSE FOUR SLAVING, VERONICA, WHILE I'M THE TOAST OF THE SCHOOL.

THE TOP PRIZE WINNER OF THE THIRD YEAR IS . . . MABEL LENTHAM!
WELL DONE, MABEL!

MABEL — WAKE UP.
EH? WHAT?

YOU FELL ASLEEP IN THE CHAIR.
YOUR FRIEND IS HERE.

POOR MABEL! DID YOU HAVE AN AWFUL TIME?
NO. ACTUALLY, IT WAS WONDERFUL! YOU AND I WERE THE TOP PUPILS IN THE SCHOOL AND THE MARYS WERE IN UTTER DISGRACE.

WHAT A PITY IT WAS ONLY A DREAM!
THE END

HOLLY RICHARDSON was really looking forward to the summer holidays —
I'M GOING TO GREECE AGAIN THIS YEAR.
I'M GOING TO FRANCE. HOW ABOUT YOU, HOLLY?
ME? OH, I'M GOING TO SPAIN!
SPAIN! ARE YOU REALLY?
THAT SURPRISED THEM! BET THEY THOUGHT I'D SAY BLACKPOOL AGAIN, BUT NOT *THIS* YEAR. SPAIN FOR TWO WHOLE WEEKS — I CAN'T WAIT! I'VE ALWAYS DREAMED OF GOING ABROAD!
HOLLY'S HOLIDAY
At home —
HOLLY — I'VE GOT SOME EXCITING NEWS!
MAYBE DAD'S GOT AN EXTRA HOLIDAY, AND WE'RE GOING FOR *THREE* WEEKS!
YOUR SISTER LUCY AND HER BOYFRIEND JACK ARE GETTING MARRIED — AND *YOU'LL* BE BRIDESMAID!
THAT'S GREAT, MUM! WHEN'S THE WEDDING?

THE END OF JULY. I'M AFRAID WE'LL HAVE TO CANCEL SPAIN. WE COULDN'T AFFORD A HOLIDAY *AND* PAY FOR LUCY'S WEDDING. STILL, NEVER MIND!
WHAT ? CANCEL OUR HOLIDAY?
YOU MIGHT NOT MIND, BUT *I* DO! OH, WHY DID LUCY HAVE TO GO AND GET MARRIED *THIS* YEAR?
HOLLY!
I DON'T WANT TO BE HER ROTTEN BRIDESMAID. WHY *SHOULD* I? SHE'S SPOILT MY FIRST HOLIDAY ABROAD. IT'S NOT *FAIR* !
Next day, at school —
LUCKY OLD YOU, HOLLY, BEING A BRIDESMAID. I'VE ALWAYS WANTED TO BE ONE!
I WAS ONE LAST YEAR, TO MY AUNTIE. I HAD GREAT FUN!
HUH! *I* WON'T!
IT'S BAD LUCK ABOUT SPAIN, THOUGH. STILL, I'M SURE YOU'LL GO NEXT YEAR!
BUT I WANTED TO GO *THIS* YEAR. NOW I'LL HAVE TO HEAR THEM ALL TALKING ABOUT ALL THEIR SUPER HOLIDAYS — AND I WON'T GET SO MUCH AS A DAY AT THE THEME PARK!
The following week —
I FEEL SILLY. OH, I *HATE* THIS WHOLE THING!
OH, THAT'S LOVELY, LUCY. YOU ARE CLEVER, MAKING YOUR OWN BRIDESMAID'S DRESS! HOLLY LOOKS SO PRETTY.

I KNOW! I'LL GET REALLY FAT SO THE STUPID DRESS WON'T FIT ON THE DAY, AND THEN I CAN'T BE A BRIDESMAID!
And so —
MORE PUDDING, HOLLY? BUT YOU'VE HAD TWO HELPINGS OF EVERYTHING ALREADY!
I KNOW, BUT I HAVEN'T GOT LONG TO GET FAT. I MUST EAT AS MUCH AS I CAN!
But, later —
OOH! I FEEL SICK AND MY TUMMY HURTS! THIS ISN'T GOING TO WORK. I'LL HAVE TO THINK OF SOMETHING ELSE.
The wedding day drew nearer.
MUM, YOU KNOW I'M IN THE JUNIOR NETBALL TEAM? WELL, WE'VE GOT A VERY IMPORTANT MATCH COMING UP A WEEK ON SATURDAY . . .
THAT'S LUCY'S WEDDING DAY! YOU'LL JUST HAVE TO TELL THE TEAM YOU CAN'T MAKE IT.
BUT I HAVE TO BE THERE! I'M THEIR TOP SCORER!
AND I SAY YOU HAVE TO BE AT YOUR SISTER'S WEDDING! WHAT'S THE MATTER WITH YOU, HOLLY? MOST GIRLS WOULD LOVE TO BE A BRIDESMAID!

AND MOST GIRLS GET TO GO ON HOLIDAYS! THERE'S ONLY A WEEK TO GO NOW — I MUST THINK OF SOMETHING. HEY, I KNOW.
Next morning —
OOOH!
HOLLY! WHAT'S WRONG?
I F-FEEL TERRIBLE, MUM. ALL HOT AND ACHEY . . . AND I'VE GOT ALL THESE SPOTS!
MY TEMPERATURE'S REALLY HIGH — I THINK IT'S MEASLES. I'LL HAVE TO BE IN QUARANTINE FOR FOURTEEN DAYS . . .
NICE TRY, YOUNG LADY, BUT I THINK IT'S AN ATTACK OF LIPSTICKITIS — AND THE ONLY KNOWN CURE IS BEING A BRIDESMAID!
Later —
WOULD YOU BELIEVE IT, LUCY? LIPSTICK SPOTS! AND SHE PROBABLY HELD THE THERMOMETER UNDER THE HOT TAP!
POOR HOLLY! I'LL TELL HER SHE DOESN'T HAVE TO BE MY BRIDESMAID.
YOU'LL DO NO SUCH THING! HOLLY'S JUST BEING SELFISH. SHE'S SULKING BECAUSE HER SPANISH HOLIDAY WAS CANCELLED.
IT'S ALL MY FAULT. IT'S A PITY I DIDN'T WIN THAT CONTEST I ENTERED IN BRIDES MONTHLY MAGAZINE, MUM. THAT WOULD HAVE SOLVED EVERYTHING!
SELFISH! SULKING! ME? LUCY'S THE ONE WHO'S BEING SELFISH, GETTING MARRIED THIS YEAR AND SPOILING OUR HOLIDAY!

But, that night —
LUCY DID LOOK UPSET THIS MORNING. I DIDN'T MEAN TO HURT HER — I GUESS MUM'S RIGHT. I HAVE BEEN THINKING ONLY OF MYSELF. I'VE BEEN A REAL PAIN!

So, next morning —
LUCY, I'VE BROUGHT YOU THE MAIL AND YOUR BREAKFAST IN BED. IT-IT'S TO SAY I'M SORRY FOR THE WAY I'VE BEEN BEHAVING.
OH, HOLLY. I'M SORRY, TOO, ABOUT YOUR HOLIDAY . . .

IT DOESN'T MATTER. WE'LL GO ANOTHER YEAR, AND I *DO* WANT TO BE YOUR BRIDESMAID, LUCY.
I AM GLAD, HOLLY. NOW WHO CAN THIS LETTER BE FROM?

Minutes later —
MUM! DAD! CANCEL THE CHURCH! CANCEL THE RECEPTION!
WHAT ? YOU MEAN YOU'RE *NOT* GETTING MARRIED?

I SURE AM! THIS IS FROM BRIDES MONTHLY — I'VE WON THE COMPETITION! THE MAGAZINE IS FLYING US ALL OUT TO *BARBADOS* FOR THE WEDDING!
BARBADOS!
OH, *LUCY* ! THIS IS WONDERFUL!

And so —
BEING A BRIDESMAID *IS* GREAT FUN, AND THIS IS THE BEST HOLIDAY EVER! I'M THE LUCKIEST GIRL IN THE WORLD!
THE END

Does CHRISTMAS drive you CRACKERS?

Or do you sail through the festive season, taking everything in your stride? Our cracking quiz will reveal all!

1. Do you always know how many days there are until Christmas?

a) Yup — even in the middle of July!
b) Not really. Not until there are only a few weeks to go.
c) Never! Christmas always sneaks up on you!

2. How long does it take you to write your Christmas cards?

a) Not long. You only send them to people who have sent cards to you!
b) Ages! There's so many to send, it can take you *weeks!*
c) You can usually have it all done in an evening.

3. What time do you get up on Christmas Day?

a) At the crack of dawn to check what's in your stocking, then you calm down and sleep a bit more.
b) You don't! You stay awake *all* night!
c) When the noise everyone else is making wakes you up!

4. Do you enjoy the school Christmas disco?

a) You hate it! It's always full of creeps armed with mistletoe. Yuk!
b) It's all right. The teachers usually make it a laugh.
c) It's one of the highlights of your year. You plan what to wear *weeks* in advance.

5. What do you do after you've opened all your presents?

a) Dive into the bath with your bubbly and stuff, don your new clothes and play with all your new things.
b) Moan, 'cos you never got what you wanted.
c) Help clear up the rubbish and check out what's on TV.

6. Are you always pleased with your Christmas presents?

a) Yes! Even if something's not quite you, it's the thought that counts!
b) No! No-one ever gets you what you ask for!
c) Usually. There's sometimes the odd thing you're not keen on, but nothing too drastic.

SCORES

1. a) 3 b) 2 c) 1   **4.** a) 1 b) 2 c) 3
2. a) 1 b) 3 c) 2   **5.** a) 3 b) 1 c) 2
3. a) 2 b) 3 c) 1   **6.** a) 3 b) 1 c) 2

Conclusions

0-8
Christmas *does* drive you crackers, which is a shame as it's the season to be jolly — or hadn't you heard? Christmas *can* actually be fun — but that's something you'll never find out if you're not prepared to join in.

9-14
You've got the balance just right! Christmas *doesn't* drive you crackers, but when it's all over, you tend to feel a bit relieved as well as disappointed — all of which is perfectly natural. So, keep up the good work!

15+
There's no chance of Christmas ever driving *you* crackers! You're the jolliest person around at Christmas — making a meal of what's only just a day, after all. Just try to remember not everyone's quite so fanatical, but they still enjoy themselves, too.

Trick or Treat?
WHEN Amy suggested that she and her friends should go out trick or treating at Hallowe'en, she had no idea what she was letting herself in for—
WHAT DO YOU THINK? WE CAN ALL GET DRESSED UP IN SPOOKY COSTUMES. IT'LL BE A LAUGH.
YEAH, OKAY!
HOW ABOUT YOU, CAROL?
SURE! I'VE GOT AN OLD WITCH'S COSTUME I WORE TO A FANCY DRESS PARTY. IT'S GOT A MASK AND EVERYTHING. I'LL WEAR THAT.
SOUNDS GREAT!
After school—
WHAT TIME WILL WE MEET UP THEN?
HOW ABOUT SIX O'CLOCK ON THE CORNER?
THAT'S FINE! I'LL SEE YOU THERE!

THIS SHEET MAKES QUITE A GOOD COSTUME. I'M REALLY LOOKING FORWARD TO TONIGHT!

And, later —
HI, TRACEY! I LIKE YOUR OUTFIT.
THANKS! YOURS IS GOOD TOO.

HERE'S CAROL!
WOW! HER WITCH COSTUME'S FANTASTIC!

LET'S GET STARTED. ON HALLOWE'EN THE WITCHES MEET, WE'VE COME TO ASK YOU . . . TRICK OR TREAT?
THAT'S ACE! I LIKE YOUR SPOOKY VOICE, CAROL.

WHERE SHALL WE GO FIRST?
I THINK WE OUGHT TO STICK TO PEOPLE WE KNOW.
YEAH! LET'S START OFF IN MY ROAD.

TRICK OR TREAT, MRS EMERY?

WHAT WONDERFUL COSTUMES, GIRLS. YOU DESERVE A TREAT. TAKE SOME OF THESE CAKES.
THANKS!
THAT'S GREAT!

WING OF BAT AND EYE OF TOAD, WE'RE TRICK OR TREATING IN THIS ROAD!
CAROL'S REALLY GOING TO TOWN ON THE POETRY TONIGHT!

NOW SHE'S PRETENDING TO CAST A WITCH'S SPELL.
YEAH. IT'S NOT LIKE HER AT ALL. USUALLY SHE'S SO QUIET. IT MUST BE BECAUSE SHE'S IN COSTUME.

Time passed quickly—
WE'VE DONE REALLY WELL TONIGHT, TRACEY. WE'VE GOT SWEETS, BISCUITS, CAKES, FRUIT *AND* MONEY!
YEAH, IT'S BEEN GREAT!

LET'S FINISH AFTER THE NEXT HOUSE, OKAY?
ALL RIGHT. I JUST WANT TO VISIT MRS WATSON. SHE HASN'T LIVED HERE LONG BUT SHE ALWAYS LOOKS LIKE SHE NEEDS CHEERING UP.

LET CAROL DO THE TALKING THEN. SHE'S THE ONE WHO'S BEEN MAKING PEOPLE LAUGH ALL NIGHT.
ALL RIGHT. COME ON, CAROL!

THAT'S ODD. SHE'S GONE!
EH? SHE CAN'T HAVE! *CAROL!*

OVER HERE!
WHERE HAVE YOU BEEN?

I'M SORRY I COULDN'T MAKE IT EARLIER, BUT I'D TO BABYSIT FOR MY SISTER. HAVE I MISSED ALL THE FUN?
WHAT ARE YOU TALKING ABOUT? YOU'VE BEEN THE LIFE AND SOUL OF THE EVENING!

HEY, WHAT HAVE YOU DONE TO YOUR COSTUME? YOUR HAT'S A DIFFERENT SHAPE.
AND THE MOON AND STARS ON YOUR CLOAK HAVE DISAPPEARED!
WHAT MOON AND STARS?

OH! YOU'RE TRICK OR TREATING. COME ON IN.
THANKS.
I'LL HAVE TO SORT THINGS OUT WITH CAROL LATER.

I'M REALLY GLAD YOU CALLED ROUND, GIRLS. I WAS THINKING ABOUT MY DAUGHTER AND FEELING A BIT UPSET. SHE DIED LAST SPRING, YOU SEE, AND I MOVED HERE TO TRY AND MAKE A FRESH START.

SHE LOVED HALLOWE'EN. THE LIFE AND SOUL OF THE EVENING, SHE WAS. THIS IS A PICTURE OF HER IN HER OUTFIT.
WHAT?

THAT'S THE GIRL TRACEY AND I JUST SPENT THE EVENING WITH! IT WASN'T CAROL AT ALL! WE'VE BEEN OUT PLAYING TRICK OR TREAT WITH A GHOST!

Phantom Pony

DENISE JACKSON was a pupil at Castle Green Boarding School —

IT'S HALF-TERM NEXT WEEK, AMY — I CAN'T WAIT! THEN I CAN GO HORSE-RIDING! I SPEND ALL MY DAYS AT THE LOCAL RIDING STABLES WHEN I'M AT HOME.

YOU'RE PONY MAD, DENISE!

THE POST'S ARRIVED!

ACE! THERE'LL BE A LETTER FROM MUM AND DAD TELLING ME WHAT TIME THEY'RE COMING TO COLLECT ME.

But —

OH!

WHAT'S THE MATTER, DENISE?

IS THAT ALL? BUT YOU CAN RIDE HERE. I HAVE A HORSE — HE'S IN THE OLD BARN OUTSIDE.
FANTASTIC! THANKS, AUNT JANE!
I'D NO IDEA MY AUNT KEPT A HORSE. THESE HOLIDAYS ARE GOING TO BE GREAT AFTER ALL!

But —
THERE ISN'T A HORSE HERE — ONLY A PILE OF JUNK. AUNT JANE MUST BE GOING DOTTY!

OH, *THIS* MUST BE WHAT SHE MEANT — A ROCKING HORSE! HUH! I'M NOT RIDING *THAT* — I'M NOT A *KID!*
HIS NAME'S RUFUS. HE'LL GIVE YOU A GOOD RIDE IF YOU LET HIM. GET ON, DEAR.

I'M GLAD MY MATES CAN'T SEE ME. OH, IF ONLY THERE WAS ANOTHER HORSE ROUND HERE — ONE THAT I COULD *REALLY* RIDE!

That night —
I CAN'T SLEEP. IT MUST BE THE STRANGE BED. OH! WHAT'S THAT NOISE?

IT'S A PONY! WHAT A BEAUTY! I MUST GO OUT AND SEE HIM.

Quickly, Denise pulled on her riding gear —
HELLO, BOY. AREN'T YOU LOVELY?
I'M SURE THE PONY'S OWNER WOULDN'T MIND ME HAVING A QUICK RIDE.

HE'S WELL CARED FOR, AND ALL TACKED UP. HIS OWNER MUST BE SOMEWHERE NEARBY.

I CAN'T SEE ANYONE THOUGH. I WON'T RIDE FAR ANYWAY.

THIS IS FANTASTIC! HE'S SO FAST — IT'S GREAT TO FEEL THE WIND IN MY HAIR.

OH! MY RIBBON'S BLOWN OFF! I'D BETTER TIE IT TO THE REINS FOR SAFE KEEPING.

Soon —
THERE, THAT'S YOU BACK SAFE AND SOUND. NOW TO FIND YOUR OWNER.

HELLO! IS THERE ANYONE HERE?

But, when Denise turned round —
HE — HE'S GONE!
WHERE ARE YOU, BOY?

Denise searched everywhere, but there was no sign of him —
HOW STRANGE! HE CAME OUT OF NOWHERE, AND NOW HE'S DISAPPEARED. IT — IT'S ALMOST AS IF HE WAS A GHOSTLY PONY.

NO! I DON'T BELIEVE IN GHOSTS. I'M SURE IT WAS A REAL PONY! AND TOMORROW I INTEND TO FIND OUT WHERE HE CAME FROM.

Next day, Denise asked round the village, but —
SORRY, DEAR. I CAN'T THINK OF ANYONE IN THE VILLAGE WITH A PONY LIKE THAT.
EVERYONE'S SAID THE SAME. BUT THE PONY MUST HAVE COME FROM SOMEWHERE!

Later —
LUNCH WON'T BE LONG. FETCH ME SOME POTATOES FROM THE BARN, WILL YOU, DENISE?
OKAY, AUNT JANE.

I'LL HAVE TO MOVE YOU TO GET TO THE POTATOES, RUFUS.

NO! I — I DON'T BELIEVE IT . . .

MY HAIR RIBBON IS TIED TO HIS REINS! SURELY RUFUS WASN'T THE PONY I RODE LAST NIGHT?

AUNT JANE SAID YOU'D GIVE ME A GOOD RIDE, IF ONLY I'D LET YOU. PERHAPS YOU USED TO CHANGE INTO A REAL PONY FOR HER, TOO, WHEN SHE WAS YOUNG.

IF I'M RIGHT, PLEASE COME TO MY WINDOW AGAIN TONIGHT, RUFUS.

WHAT WAS THAT NOISE? IT SOUNDED LIKE A PONY NEIGHING. SOMETHING TELLS ME THESE HOLIDAYS AREN'T GOING TO BE BORING AFTER ALL!
THE END

THE COMP

IT was two weeks before the end of the Christmas term. And "Grim Gertie" Grimstyle had news for Form 3B of Redvale Comprehensive!

YOU HAVE MY BED, SUZIE, I'LL TAKE THE CAMP BED. I'VE EMPTIED TWO DRAWERS AND HALF THE WARDROBE FOR YOU. NEED ANY HELP UNPACKING?
NO, THANKS, LAURA. IT'S REALLY GOOD OF YOU TO MOVE ALL YOUR STUFF FOR ME.

WHAT'S SHE LIKE, THEN?
SHE'S EVER SO QUIET, HAYLEY. SHE READS TONS. SHE SPENT MOST OF THE EVENING IN OUR ROOM WITH A BOOK. IT'LL BE DIFFERENT ON MONDAY, THOUGH.
HOW COME?

HER MUM DOESN'T WANT HER TO MISS ANY SCHOOL, SO SHE'S SPENDING THE LAST FEW DAYS OF TERM AT THE COMP, WITH US.
GEE, THAT'S TOUGH! SHE MUST'VE BEEN HOPING SHE'D HAVE AN EXTRA-LONG CHRISTMAS HOLIDAY!

At Laura's —
IT'S GREAT NEWS ABOUT YOUR MUM DOING SO WELL IN HOSPITAL, SUZIE.
HEY, YOU WANT TO JOIN OUR DANCE GROUP?
OH, NO! I CAN'T DANCE. I-I'LL JUST WATCH.

ONE TWO THREE TURN FIVE SIX SEVEN KICK . . .
SUZIE'S REALLY WATCHING. SHE SEEMS TO LIKE IT. SHAME SHE CAN'T DANCE.

On Monday —
LIKE A CRISP, SUZIE?
THIS WAY FOR THE GUIDED TOUR OF THE TORTURE CHAMBER!
CLAIRE AND NIKKI AND EVERYONE ARE BEING REALLY NICE TO SUZIE, BUT SHE JUST SMILES AND HARDLY SAYS ANYTHING. I'VE NEVER KNOWN ANYONE SO MOUSY!

In Art —
IT'S FINISHED — SOOTY COLE'S IN FOR A SURPRISE!
YEAH — CAN'T WAIT TO SEE HIS FACE!
WHAT ARE THOSE TWO UP TO?

IT'S HENRY, THE SCHOOL SKELETON!
QUICK! GET INTO YOUR SEATS. WE'LL ASK SOOTY FOR SOMETHING FROM THE CUPBOARD!
HE'S A BIT ON THE BONY SIDE FOR SANTA! HA-HA!

But —
AH, MR COLE. COULD I HAVE A BOX OF PENCILS, PLEASE?
CERTAINLY, MISS GRIMSTYLE. HELP YOURSELF — THEY'RE IN THE CUPBOARD.
WHAT? OH, NO!

EEEEAGH!

WHOSE STUPID, CHILDISH IDEA OF A JOKE IS THIS?
ER — AHEM! I'M SURE IT'S ALL IN FUN, MISS GRIMSTYLE. AFTER ALL, IT IS CHRISTMAS . . .

At last, Mr Cole succeeded in calming her down —
HA! DID YOU SEE GERTIE'S FACE?
IT WAS BRILLIANT!
EVEN BETTER THAN CATCHING SOOTY!

ALL RIGHT, DAVID HODGSON AND JOHN FREDERICKS! YOU'D BETTER PUT THAT SKELETON BACK IN THE BIO LAB WHERE HE BELONGS — WITHOUT HIS SANTA SUIT. I'M CONFISCATING THAT TILL THE END OF TERM!
EH? HOW DID HE KNOW?

SOOTY'S A GOOD SPORT, ISN'T HE, CLAIRE?
YEAH, NIK. HE WAS REALLY STRUGGLING NOT TO LAUGH HIMSELF WHEN HE SAW GERTIE'S FACE!
SUZIE LAUGHED HER SOCKS OFF THEN. MAYBE SHE'S NOT SO SHY AND MOUSY AFTER ALL . . .

That night —
HEY — THAT SOUNDS LIKE OUR DANCE MUSIC. WHAT'S GOING ON? HAVE ROZ AND THE TWINS COME OVER WHILE I WAS AT THE LIBRARY?

SUZIE! SO — THAT'S WHY SHE DIDN'T WANT TO COME TO THE LIBRARY WITH ME!

OH! L-LAURA. I — I D-DIDN'T KNOW YOU WERE THERE! I THOUGHT EVERYONE WAS OUT.
SUZIE, THAT WAS BRILLIANT! YOU'VE LEARNED NEARLY EVERY STEP OF OUR DANCE — JUST FROM WATCHING US. GO ON!

NO, I C-CAN'T. I CAN NEVER DANCE A STEP IF I KNOW ANYONE'S WATCHING. I FEEL STUPID. I CAN ONLY EVER DANCE . . . FOR ME.
BUT YOU'RE GOOD! SUZIE, JOIN OUR GROUP. YOU COULD DANCE IN THE CONCERT WITH US!

NO! I TOLD YOU . . . I CAN'T! NOT ON A STAGE WITH PEOPLE LOOKING. I KNOW I'D BE HOPELESS. I'M SORRY, LAURA, BUT THANKS FOR ASKING.
BUT SHE ISN'T HOPELESS — NOT AT ALL! OH, WELL, I CAN'T PUSH IT, I SUPPOSE.

I'M NOT KIDDING YOU, ROZ. SHE HAD NEARLY EVERY STEP OF OUR DANCE BY HEART . . .
COME OFF IT, LAURA. IF SHE WAS THAT BRILLIANT, SHE WOULDN'T BE SHY ABOUT IT!

THOUGHT UP AN ACT YOU CAN DO YET, HODGE?
I KNOW. YOU'RE GOING TO BE CLOWNS!
IT'S A SECRET. BUT IT'S GOING TO BE A SHOWSTOPPER!

IN OTHER WORDS, YOU DON'T KNOW WHAT YOU'RE GOING TO DO YET!
OH, YES, WE DO! WE'RE . . .
PSST! HODGE! DON'T TELL 'EM, MAKE 'EM WAIT!
BOTHER. ALMOST GOT IT OUT OF HIM!

The day before the concert —
YOU GUYS ARE LATE! HEY, HAYLEY — WHAT HAPPENED TO YOUR KNEE? IT'S BLEEDING.
SHE CAME OFF HER BIKE.
IT'S NOT BAD. I'LL JUST WASH IT AND STICK A PLASTER ON. IT'LL BE OKAY.

HOW DO WE LOOK, SUZIE?
REALLY GOOD.

SUZIE'S WATCHED US EVERY TIME WE'VE REHEARSED — IT'S LIKE SHE REALLY DOES WANT TO JOIN IN, BUT SHE DAREN'T.
HAYLEY? WHAT'S UP?
OH, MY KNEE'S A BIT SORE NOW . . .

And, after lunch –
LAURA — BAD NEWS. HAYLEY'S KNEE'S REALLY SWOLLEN AND SORE AFTER ALL OUR DANCING. SHE'S GOT A NASTY BRUISE TOO. SHE SAYS IT'S SO PAINFUL, THERE'S NO WAY SHE CAN DANCE!
WHAT? BUT THE CONCERT'S TOMORROW!

SUZIE, WILL YOU HELP US OUT?
TAKE HAYLEY'S PLACE? NO! I TOLD YOU — I CAN'T! YOU CAN DO THE DANCE WITH JUST THE THREE OF YOU . . . PLEASE, LAURA!

WE CAN'T. YOU KNOW THAT! IT HAS TO BE WITH FOUR. PLEASE, SUZIE — FOR MY SAKE? IT'S ONLY IN OUR SCHOOL HALL AND IT'S FOR A GOOD CAUSE!
WELL, I — I'LL TRY. BUT I KNOW I'LL BE TERRIBLE.

So Laura called Roz and Becky round —
AND I THOUGHT LAURA WAS KIDDING!
WOW! SUZIE REALLY CAN DO OUR DANCE!
YOU KEEP THIS UP, SUZIE, AND IT WON'T BE HODGE AND FREDDY WHO ARE THE STARS OF THE SHOW!

Next day —
I — I SHOULD N-NEVER HAVE SAID I'D DO IT. I C-CAN'T. I FEEL S-SICK.
WE'VE ALL GOT BUTTERFLIES, SUZIE. THAT'S NATURAL! LET'S GO TO THE WINGS AND WATCH THE OTHER ACTS. "MY-MUM-SAYS" MARGARET'S ON!

"OH, DON'T DECEIVE ME, OH, NEVER LEAVE ME, HOW COULD YOU USE A POOR MAIDEN SO!"
MARGARET'S GOT A NICE VOICE, I SUPPOSE — EVEN IF HER SONGS ARE A BIT BORING. STILL, THE OLD FOLKS SEEM TO LIKE THEM.

TA-DAAA! AND NOW — PRESENTING — THE GREAT FREDERICO!
SO THAT'S THEIR BIG SECRET — A MAGIC ACT! "THE GREAT FREDERICO" — OH, BROTHER! THIS SHOULD BE A LAUGH.

MY ASSISTANT TEARS THE PAPER INTO A THOUSAND PIECES AND TIPS IT INTO THE HAT.
. . . AND, HEY PRESTO, THE PAPER IS WHOLE AND COMPLETE AGAIN.

LIKE SO — OOPS!
IT WORKED BEFORE!
HA, HA, HA, HA!

AHEM! FOR MY NEXT TRICK — THE AMAZING SOLID WATER! I TURN THE GLASS UPSIDE DOWN . . . I REMOVE THE CARD . . . AND THE WATER . . .

. . . STAYS IN THE GLASS. OO-ER!
GLUB!
HEE, HEE, HEE! HO, HO!

I'M TELLING YOU THOSE TRICKS ALL WORKED BEFORE! THOSE GIRLS PUT ME OFF WITH THEIR GIGGLING.
THAT'S THE LAST TIME I DO A MAGIC ACT WITH YOU, MATE!
THE 'GREAT' FREDERICO. HA, HA, HA!

Suddenly it was the girls' turn —
SUZIE'S DOING GREAT!
THEY — THEY LIKE US! THEY'RE STARTING TO CLAP ALONG.

YOU LOT WERE REALLY GOOD!
IT WAS FUN! I STOPPED FEELING SICK AS SOON AS I WAS UP THERE. AND I DID IT, DIDN'T I? I DANCED IN FRONT OF ALL THOSE PEOPLE!
YOU SURE DID, SUZIE! YOU KNOW, YOU SHOULD TAKE UP DANCE — JOIN A CLASS OR SOMETHING!

I THINK I'D LIKE THAT, ROZ!
I DON'T THINK MY MOUSY COUSIN WILL BE QUITE SO SHY IN FUTURE. SHE'S GOT SOME CONFIDENCE NOW . . . THANKS TO YOU, HAYLEY!
ME? WHY ME?

I WAS JUST WONDERING HOW BAD YOUR LEG WAS? I MEAN, WHEN YOU WALKED IN JUST NOW, YOU'D LOST YOUR LIMP, BANDAGE OR NO BANDAGE!
AHEM! WELL! WE HAD TO SEE IF YOU WERE RIGHT ABOUT SUZIE, DIDN'T WE? AND YOU WERE!
HEY, EVERYONE — LOOK AT SOOTY COLE!

HO! HO! HO! MERRY CHRISTMAS!
OUR SANTA SUIT! SO *THAT'S* WHY HE CONFISCATED IT!
YOU HAVE TO ADMIT, HODGE — HE SUITS IT A LOT BETTER THAN HENRY DID! HA, HA!
THE END

DRAWING PINS
It's Buster — he's her little dog.
He's got his chance to star.
She's pinned him right above her bed,
'Cos *he's* her fave, by far!